DIRTY ROCKER BOYS

DIRTY ROCKER BOYS

Love and Lust
on the Sunset Strip

BOBBIE BROWN

WITH CAROLINE RYDER

GALLERY BOOKS G

NEW YORK   LONDON   TORONTO   SYDNEY   NEW DELHI

G

Gallery Books
A Division of Simon & Schuster, Inc.
1230 Avenue of the Americas
New York, NY 10020

First Gallery Books hardcover edition December 2013

GALLERY BOOKS and colophon are registered trademarks of Simon & Schuster, Inc.

For information about special discounts for bulk purchases, please contact Simon & Schuster Special Sales at 1-866-506-1949 or business@ simonandschuster.com.

The Simon & Schuster Speakers Bureau can bring authors to your live event. For more information or to book an event contact the Simon & Schuster Speakers Bureau at 1-866-248-3049 or visit our website at www.simonspeakers.com.

Interior design by Julie Schroeder

Manufactured in the United States of America

10 9 8 7 6 5 4 3 2 1

Library of Congress Cataloging-in-Publication Data
Brown, Bobbie, 1969–
  Dirty rocker boys : love and lust on the Sunset Strip / Bobbie Brown with Caroline Ryder.
  p. cm.
  Summary: "An uncensored Hollywood tell-all filled with explicit tales of love, sex, and revenge from the video vixen made famous by Warrant's rock anthem 'Cherry Pie.'"—Provided by publisher.
  1. Brown, Bobbie, 1969- 2. Actors—United States—Biography. 3. Rock musicians' spouses—United States—Biography. 4. Models (Persons)—United States—Biography. I. Ryder, Caroline. II. Title.
  PN2287.B6965A3 2013
  791.4302'8092—dc23
  [B]
                              2013026429

ISBN 978-1-4767-3470-5
ISBN 978-1-4767-3473-6 (ebook)

I would like dedicate this book to my family;
Mom, Dad, Taylar, Adam, Mr. Bill, Mr. Earl,
Jani, and the Ex-Wives of Rock *family.*

CONTENTS

Chapter One
COCK OF AGES

EX-WIFE OF ROCK

Wait, *what* happened? Last week, Tommy Lee was my fiancé. This week, he's married. To Pamela Anderson.

It was February 1995, and in the aftermath of Tommy's shotgun wedding on the beach in Cancún, four days after our breakup, my coping strategy was twofold.

1. Get high.

I had a line on some of the dopest trucker speed in Malibu. It was a killer buzz, lasting for days—back in 1995, the meth was clean as a bean. I had been secretly using throughout my relationship with Tommy, as a way to maintain the rail-thin Barbie-doll figure that Tommy liked, and as a way to escape the growing sense that my life was fucked-up, on all levels. Very few people knew about my little problem, even though my pupils were dilated in broad daylight and I shouted at invisible dogs. I drove to the corner store for soda, came back eight hours later with gardening tools. My glitter gun became my best friend as I embarked on endlessly elaborate middle-of-the-night crafting projects, just to give my racing mind something to focus on. I was spun, a member of a long-established club known as the "Hollywood Speed Freak Society"—a long line of celebrity tweakers who, like me, were afflicted by a cursed disposition for that unsavory mistress, methamphetamine.

2. Get even.

A few years prior, a voodoo doctor in my native Louisiana had warned me about messing with revenge. Dark energy, he said, "will come back and bite you." But after seven years of having my heart shredded by Sunset Strip cock rockers, I wanted to teach those assholes a lesson. *I'm going to flip the script, treat the guys the way they treat us,* I thought. I had reached my tipping point. I was ripe for revenge.

I looked in the mirror. Twenty-six years old. My peroxide mane was messy; my roots were showing. I was Courtney Love meets Malibu Barbie, with the gaunt yet chic figure of a runway model—around ninety-five pounds on a fat day. *Thank you, crystal.* The world knew me as Bobbie Brown, fiancée of Tommy Lee, ex-wife of Jani Lane, cutie-patootie from the "Cherry Pie" video on MTV. They'd yet to experience Bobbie Brown, wrathful, world-weary drug addict with no pride left to lose. I put on lipstick, a Wonderbra, and some assless chaps. I was ready to hit the clubs.

After a year playing Malibu Rapunzel, holed up in Tommy Lee's beachfront fortress, I couldn't wait to fall back into Hollywood's welcoming arms. I had always been a club kid. I loved the darkness, the anonymity, the feeling of being underground.

The velvet ropes that melted as soon as I arrived. Tommy may have tossed me aside, but in clubland, I was still queen.

In 1995, Thursday nights at Grand Ville were where it was at. The club was a hub of the '90s neo-burlesque scene, full of corseted girls with shoe-polish-black hair, a whirl of rhinestones, glitter, and feathers. Grand Ville was the toughest door in town, but the promoter, Rick Calamaro, a dear friend of mine (may he rest in peace), always greeted me with a smile.

"Welcome back, Bobbie."

I stepped inside, through the looking glass, and into a different reality. A pleasure dome, decadent and carnivalesque. Everywhere I turned, I saw the ghosts of my past loves. There were the Tommy Lees—wild, tattooed romantics, who turn mean when the roses wilt. The Jani Lanes—sweet, tortured artists weighed down by their demons. The Matthew Nelsons—blond angels destined to fly away. The exes in my life are no different to the exes in any girl's life—except mine all happened to be rock stars.

Who better to confide in about my problems than a wide-eyed actor named Leonardo DiCaprio, who had about as much life experience as a Care Bear? "Thing is," I told him as we chatted at the club, "if you're not grown-up enough to deal with their 'musician issues,' then rock star lovers can send a girl down some very dark and dangerous rabbit holes. You know what I mean?"

Leo did not know what I meant. We were in the VIP lounge

at Grand Ville, and he was looking at me like I was insane. I *was* insane, kind of. The stress of being married to one rock star (Jani Lane), engaged to another (Tommy Lee), and then jilted thanks to my professional rival (Pamela Anderson) had taken a toll. I was tired, jaded, defeated. The speed was playing tricks on my sanity, and my behavior had grown notoriously unpredictable. But how could Leo possibly understand? He was so fresh and upbeat. He looked like he should be drinking milk, not martinis.

For years Leo had been dancing up to me at the clubs, saying how he wanted to make me his girlfriend. I smiled and patted him on the head. *How cute.* I was seven years his senior and felt like his grandma. I'd never been someone's G.I.L.F. before. "Do you think it's too *Harold and Maude* if I do it with Leo?" I asked Sharise Neil, ex-wife of Mötley Crüe's Vince Neil, and my sister in pleasure seeking. Sharise raised an eyebrow and shrugged. At least baby-faced Leo had a grown-up career, I thought. *The Basketball Diaries*, his breakthrough movie, had come out that year, and he was about to star in Baz Luhrmann's *Romeo + Juliet*. If I hooked up with Leo, who was younger, cuter, and about to be more famous than Tommy Lee, it would hit Tommy right in the ballsack.

This time, when Leo came dancing up to me, I played along. "Call me, I dare you." My inner G.I.L.F. was ready to party.

UNICORNS AND UNIBROWS

I opened my front door, and there he was, wide face, cornflower-blue eyes, big smile. Leo's hair was pulled back in barrettes and he was wearing a headband. He looked pretty, like a ballerina. I invited him in. "Can I put on some music?" he asked, waving a CD in the air.

"Sure."

Don't go chasing waterfalls.
Please stick to the rivers and the lakes that you're used to.

Leo sat on the floor, eyes closed, singing along. I recognized the song, by that R & B girl band TLC. It was all over the radio. I stood there for a while, watching Leo sing along, wondering what to do next, and what conversation there was to make. There was none. Pokémon? New Kids on the Block? College? "Let's go to the bedroom." I said. Leo nodded.

My bed was big and tall, and you had to climb up a small ladder to get to it. "You want to get up there with me, Leo?"

"Okay!"

We started kissing. I pulled his T-shirt over his head, leaving the barrettes in his hair. I unbuttoned his jeans and tugged down on his boxers. What I saw made me gasp. It made no sense. The kid put Tommy Lee to shame. "Wow, Leo, I wasn't expecting that." Next to his slim body, his assets were startlingly huge. "Wait, let me turn the light on," I said. "I've got to see this properly." Yup, even under closer inspection, Leonardo DiCaprio's crotch was on steroids. I couldn't take my eyes off it. *Ha, wait till Tommy "I've got the biggest dick in Hollywood" hears about this,* I thought.

"So, Bobbie, do you have any diseases?"

Oh.

The question dropped like ice water on my head. I hadn't really thought about it. I'd come of age on the Sunset Strip, which was basically a glorified STD factory. No one in the rock scene wore condoms. *No one.* Had I been tested? Of course not. Nothing *seemed* too diseased down there, but I hadn't thought to ask a doctor to check me out. On the Strip, when it came to bodily juices, sharing was caring.

"Also, Bobbie, what about gonorrhea? Have you been tested for that? And when you suck my dick, can you do it with a condom on?" *Gah, he's so PC,* I thought.

Truth be told, I could hardly blame Leo for feeling the safe-sex vibe with me. Tommy Lee was one of the biggest man-whore stripper chasers on the Strip. But I had never sucked anyone's wiener with a condom on it before. *Oh well, first time for everything.*

Leo rolled a rubber on, lay back, and closed his eyes. My cue to get started. I kissed his belly and drew him close to me. I began to lick and kiss his gargantuan penis. I tried to put it in my mouth. I could barely breathe. My jaw locked; my eyeballs bulged. So I went back to licking it. Unfortunately, the latex tasted like the inside of a balloon, bitter, reminiscent of trips to the dentist. I rode my tongue up and down, trying to ignore the acrid taste, but after a few minutes, I had to stop. The flavor, along with his spectacular girthyness, was making me gag.

"Leo, I'm sorry but this condom tastes terrible. I don't think I can do it." Leo pulled me down next to him and kissed me sweetly. "You're right, that does taste kinda funny." I pulled him on top of me. His eyes stayed open, gazing into mine. His brow furrowed a little as he eased himself into me. I inhaled sharply—he was . . . *titanic*.

"Wow, Leo, that's nice, really nice." Waves of satisfaction rippled through my body. I pulled Leo deeper into me, as deep as he could go. Revenge was sweeter than I could have imagined. If only Tommy Lee could see me now.

"Wait. Wait a second. Don't move, Bobbie," whispered Leo.

"What's wrong?"

"We need to slow down."

"Um, okay."

We were about one minute into the lovemaking. I waited a few beats. I pulled him close again and he squeaked.

"No, no, not yet."

I looked at Leo's perfect face as he grimaced, hoping to make it past the two-minute mark. He was a unicorn. Rare, innocent, and horny. Me, on the other hand, I'd been engaged, married, and had given birth. I needed a man, not a man-child.

Ah what's the point?

"I'm going to get a drink," I said, pushing him off me, climbing down out of the bed, throwing on a T-shirt. I was mad at him, mad at the whole world. The speed was making me antsy, bitchy, and annoyed with the handsome young golden boy for making me feel like a pedophile. Heading down the stairs, I yelled over my shoulder. "Maybe you should take your socks off next time." Leo seemed confused. "Okay . . . can you make me a drink too?"

"How about a glass of milk?"

I went downstairs and hung out by myself, watching TV. I just wanted him gone. "Bobbie? Are you coming back?" I heard him call from my bedroom.

"Nah."

Leo, at his tender age, had yet to learn how to recognize damaged goods. How was he to know he was just one in a series of revenge fucks? A little confused by my behavior, Leo got up, got dressed, and left.

A few months later, I did an interview on the radio in which I mentioned Leo's extraordinary penis. Leo, apparently, didn't see the funny side. He sent his best friend Kevin Connolly, who you might have seen on *Entourage* and in the movie *He's Just Not That Into You*, over to talk to me. Kevin was a mutual friend of ours who I talked to on the phone occasionally, and who had also asked me out a few times. Today, though, he was visiting on "official business."

"Yeah, so Leo heard about that interview you did," said Kevin. "He's really pissed off that you would talk about something personal on-air."

"I'm sorry," I said, stifling my laughter. I couldn't imagine Tommy ever getting mad about the world knowing what a huge penis he has. But then, Leo wasn't a cock-rock musician. For all his playfulness, he was a serious kid. I never heard from him again. Which was fine by me.

Next!

A few weeks later, the actor Stephen Dorff sidled up to me on the dance floor at Grand Ville, with an entourage of about six dudes. *Wow, he really thinks he's the shit.* I towered over him in my heels and had to bend down to hear what he was saying.

"So, you wanna go back to my house and fuck?" said Stephen, in my ear. No hello, no "how are you?" Just straight to business.

"Excuse me?"

He leaned in a little closer, and I could feel his spit on my cheek.

"Do you want to go back to my place?"

You picked the wrong ice queen, motherfucker, I thought. I hit him with the most withering up-and-down stare I could muster and proceeded to tear him a new one.

"Well, first of all, you're short. Second of all, you're fat. And third of all, you have a fucking unibrow." I made a unibrow above my nose with two fingers, to illustrate. "Oh, and you're spitting on me. Can you back the fuck up? Yeah, get out of here, chubby."

Damn. After all these years of being fun, goofy Bobbie Brown, unleashing my inner asshole felt *good.* Damn the consequences—these guys had it coming. Thanks to the heart-numbing properties of the speed I was on, I had no mercy. Stephen turned to his entourage, stunned. "Come on, guys, let's go." Sharise, who had seen the whole encounter, was about to die of laughter. "What a dork!" she giggled. Fresh off her divorce from Vince, she was as disillusioned with men as I was. "Let's show those assholes," I said.

Next stop, Kevin Costner's house. I looked around the party—five guys and about a hundred girls. I wandered through the house and peered into a bedroom. Kevin was sitting on the bed, encircled by females. *Oh, please,* I thought.

"Come on in," he said, smiling.

I sat down on the bed. The girl sitting next to me put her legs around her neck. One leg, and then the other.

"This one's a sure thing," I said, rolling my eyes. Kevin seemed amused. "You're funny," he said. He asked me for my number, and as I jotted down my digits on a napkin, I giggled privately. *Mwa-ha-ha-ha.* If only Kevin knew what he was about to get himself into. He called me the next night. "Hey, Bobbie, are you in front of your TV? Check out channel five." I put it on. *Dances with Wolves.* "Well, hi . . . there you are." My eyes rolled deep into the back of my head.

"You girls should come to a party in Malibu this weekend. There will be music and dancing. You'll love it." I wasn't sure I could be bothered. Kevin's over-earnest egotism was turning me off, but Sharise wanted to go. *Ah, fuck it.* Ready for a good time, we made the hour's drive to Malibu from her house in the Valley, singing Sheryl Crow songs all the way.

Malibu's twenty-seven-mile stretch of sun-drenched coastline is home to Mel Gibson, Steven Spielberg, Courteney Cox, and dotted with glassy million-dollar homes that stare out at the surf. But behind the elegant façades lies the same hedonistic, morally bankrupt scene you'll find in Hollywood—guys in Ferraris, strung-out Bel Air wives, rockers in cowboy boots, dust clouds of cocaine in their wake. *Idiots*, I thought, taking a quick key bump of speed in the car. I *hated* coke. Coke was for losers.

Sharise and I walked into the party and headed straight for the dance floor. The DJ was spinning some rad hip-hop, and thanks to the speed, I had plenty of energy. I tuned into the rhythm, oblivious to the curious gazes of the other partygoers as Sharise and I busted out our raddest '90s dance moves, pop-locking, voguing, and doing the Running Man like it was going out of style (which it was). Then I felt something behind me; it was Kevin, dancing up to me, awkward mating ritual in full effect. Imagine someone being led by his penis in a pelvic thrust, off the beat, headed in your direction. Instinctively, I shoved him with both arms across the dance floor.

"Whoa," said Kevin, stumbling. Undeterred, he came back at me with that pelvis.

"Why don't you go dance somewhere else?" I sniped.

Sharise told me to stop being a bitch. I'll admit, I was kind of an asshole back in those days. I was not impressed by any-body or anything, no matter how many Oscars or Grammys they might have. Which always seemed to make them come on stronger. Sharise begged me to please just be nice to Kevin—she was always a tad more compassionate and polite than I—so when he invited us over to his house to watch a movie the fol-lowing night, I gave it one more shot.

DANCES WITH DISASTERS

Kevin opened the door, wearing a country-western-type outfit: blue jeans and a plaid shirt. He had a beautiful Spanish-style home in the Hollywood Hills that he had bought from Richard Dreyfuss.

"Hello, girls."

Within moments of arriving I managed to smash my glass of vodka tonic on the tile floor. I was notoriously clumsy, always tripping, crashing, breaking things, possessed by inexplicable involuntary spasms. I was embarrassed, so I grabbed Sharise's glass and threw it on the floor too.

"It's a Greek restaurant! O-pa!"

"No, it's not a Greek restaurant, Bobbie," said Kevin, dryly. *Ugh, what a bore,* I thought.

"Whatever."

I was more off-kilter than usual, having been up all night partying with the guys from Coal Chamber. Pierced nü-metal goth kids in black eyeliner, they were my kind of people, with my kind of taste in vices. Normally, I found it easy to hop between the rock scene and glitzy Hollywood shit, but the night I showed up at Kevin's tastefully appointed home, my brain was clearly still in heavy metal parking lot mode.

Turning a blind eye to the shards of Waterford crystal on the floor tile, Kevin suggested we retire to the film-viewing room, where he had a movie cued up for us to watch. I stepped into the viewing room, looking back over my shoulder to say something to Sharise, failing to notice the rather large step in front of me. I went flying, landing face-first on the ground. Man, why was this always happening to me?

"*Face-plant!*" I yelled, chewing on a mouthful of freshly shampooed carpet.

For Kevin, the horror of my dangerous one-woman freak show was starting to sink in. He looked nervous. "What the fuck is wrong with you?" hissed Sharise.

We sat down on the wraparound banquette in his screening room and Kevin put on the movie. *EDtv.* I tried to relax and act like a normal human being, but something about the way Woody Harrelson delivered his lines was really pissing me off. He kept stuttering and blinking his eyes. "Fuck!" I exclaimed at the top of my voice, in full Tourette's mode, not realizing I was thinking out loud.

"What?"

"The fuck? He did it again. This is ridiculous."

"What's the matter?" said Kevin, pausing the film.

"I-I-I don't know, K-K-Kevin." I imitated Woody, stuttering and blinking my eyes. Kevin looked at me blankly.

"Woody Harrelson keeps stuttering every time he delivers. It's pissing me off."

"Can't you maybe ignore it?"

"No."

"Please just shut up, Bobbie," said Sharise. Kevin put the movie back on. In the very next scene, Woody Harrelson stuttered and blinked. Again.

"Oh. You're right," said Kevin, sounding irritated. "I can't watch the movie now. Perhaps we should just turn it off." Sharise, ever the peacemaker, convinced him it would be okay to carry on watching, so long as we tried not to focus too much on Woody's tics. I couldn't be bothered and drifted into a deep, twitchy sleep, for the first time in days. The speed was starting to wear off.

"Wake up, Bobbie! The movie's over," said Sharise. I was hanging off the couch sideways, a little drool dangling from my lips.

"Let's all go upstairs for a nightcap, shall we?" said Kevin, in one last desperate bid to rescue the evening. "There's a magnificent view of the city from my bedroom." Kudos to Kevin for not kicking me out. Seriously. Hats off. I guess he must have really wanted to get laid. He led the way up to his bedroom, which, as promised, had an enormous deck overlooking the whole of Hollywood. I stepped out on to it, inhaling the heady scent of eucalyptus and orange blossom, mesmerized by the snaking glow of the freeways in the distance. The balcony railing was only crotch-high, and as I leaned over, I half stumbled and gasped, holding on tight to make sure I didn't flip over and tumble down the hillside below.

"Whoa, kind of dangerous over here!" I yelled at Kevin and Sharise, who were ignoring me. Since Tommy had left me, I'd been on a string of dates, most of them calamitous, or hilarious. Something inside me had become resistant to all that was sane and decent in this world. I was a chaos magnet, a bad-luck charm, a catastrophe in kitten heels. Sharise, too, had suffered her fair share of rock-wife damage, but, unlike me, she could keep it together in public.

"Maybe you should go inside—you're making me nervous," called over Kevin.

"Okay, but I want a cigarette," I said, strolling into the bedroom. I lit up my Marlboro and looked around. The room was huge, shaped like an octagon, with a giant fireplace illuminating one of the walls.

"No smoking inside," I heard Kevin call from the balcony.

"Bob, he said no smoking," Sharise hollered.

"All right, all right," I said, taking one last pull on my cigarette. *Where do I put the fucker out?* I thought, eyes searching for an ashtray.

I flipped the cigarette toward the crackling fire—*fliiiiick*—and walked back toward the balcony, trying to join in the conversation. Moments later, Kevin's expression shifted. He pointed behind me, shaking his head, panic in his eyes.

"My bedroom's on fire."

I turned around, and indeed, flames were crawling up the wall from the mantel above the fireplace, where my cigarette had landed.

"Holy shit!" I ran into the bedroom, took off my jacket, and slapped it against the wall, trying to put out the flames. Sparks exploded like it was the Fourth of July.

"Dude, stop fanning the flames! You're making it worse!" Sharise hissed.

"I am *so* sorry, Kevin!" I said, determined to put out the blaze. I took off my scarf and slapped at the wall. Even after the fire went out, I carried on slapping and thrashing, grunting like a tennis player as I gave the wall a good beating. Kevin's face was stricken.

"Will you fucking calm down," yelled Sharise. I turned to my friend, annoyed at her constant chiding, and tried to whip-slap her in the face with the tail end of my burnt-up scarf. Except I missed and ended up slapping Kevin in the eyeball instead. On the snapback, it ricocheted into my face.

"Jesus! Ouch!"

"Fuck! Sorry, Kevin!"

I was squinting. Kevin's face was sooty, and he was cupping one eye. His fancy mantelpiece was charred and ashy. Sharise's jaw, as it so often was when we hung out, was on the ground.

"Bobbie, where on God's Earth did you come from?" said Kevin, shaking his head.

Chapter Two

BYE-BYE, MISS AMERICAN PIE

Baton Rouge, Louisiana, 1968

According to family lore, it was stickier than molasses the day my dad told my mom she was the finest piece of ass in the South, prompting my mom to fling the contents of her ice cream soda in his face. "Maybe this'll cool you down!" she yelled, and my dad cracked a smile, squinting through the root beer blur. *My kinda girl,* he thought, licking his lips. It was the first time Bobby Gene Brown and Judy Ann Faul had met, and frankly, with the heat, a little ice cream soda in the face was not entirely unrefreshing. Bobby eyed Judy up and down—she was seventeen and a half, with cat-eye makeup and jet-black hair, just like Priscilla Presley. He wiped down his leather jacket with a napkin and watched my mother storm out of the diner, picturing her in a leopard-print bikini.

"She's gonna be my wife," he said to the cashier, who shook his head.

Three months later, they were married.

Bobby was nine years older than Judy, a wrong-side-of-the-tracks kind of guy, a diamond in the rough with dark hair, full lips, and blue eyes. He grew up in Spartanburg, South Carolina, a quaint Southern backwater founded by French fur trappers and pioneers, and dotted with church steeples and apple orchards. Straight out of school he enlisted in the military but never served. He decided to become a car salesman, and let's just say, whatever the clichés are about a man who sells used cars, they're pretty much true, especially when it came to my daddy. He had the gift of gab and was smooth enough to talk a good Catholic girl like my mom into giving a guy like him the time of day.

My mom, Judy, grew up in a Catholic family in a small swampy town named Church Point, Louisiana, so-called Cajun Music Capital of the World. She was one of six, raised by a single mother, third from the youngest. She was born sick, with spinal meningitis, so my grandma Isabelle used to make her wear a braid necklace that had been dipped in holy water, to make her get well. I don't know if it was Jesus or just good fortune that did it, but my mother did grow into a healthy, beautiful teenager.

My grandpa had walked out on my grandma when all their children were kids, so my grandma raised the six of them on her own. With such a big family, the children had to go out to work early—when she was thirteen, my mom lied about her age to get a job at a store called Shoe Town. With so little money in the family, she had to grow up quick.

When Bobby Brown started showing up at the house with big bags of groceries, Judy and Isabelle liked that. Money was tight, and groceries were always welcome. They were then living in Baton Rouge, capital of Louisiana, the quiet cousin of New Orleans. It's nice and simple there, and so are the people.

"Miss Judy, Miss Isabelle . . . I saw some wonderfully fresh meats at the store today. I couldn't help thinking you might want some for your sandwiches."

"Bless your heart," said my grandma, eyeing the grocery bags, handing my mother a cigarette, and mouthing, *I like him.*

When Bobby choked Judy in a jealous rage during one of their first dates, Judy assumed his actions were a sign of his passion for her. After three months of dating, they married. A year later, on October 7, 1969, I was born, following a grueling twenty-six-hour labor. "You were a bitch coming into this world, and you still are," my mom likes to joke. "Let's call her Bobbie Jean," said my mom proudly, cradling me in her arms in the delivery room. She was eighteen. My dad liked that— Bobby Gene Brown's firstborn child would be named Bobbie Jean Brown, after him.

We lived in a house on Pioneer Drive, in the Park Forest subdivision of Baton Rouge. It was a quaint little neighborhood, with a community pool where all the kids would ride their bikes and go swimming in the summertime. I enrolled at the elementary school down the street, Park Forest Elementary, and played hopscotch with all the neighbors' kids. From the outside, life looked pretty sweet.

My mom always wanted me to be pretty. She imagined me as a princess or a Southern debutante, and was always fixing my hair, pulling it into a tight ponytail or putting it in rollers before bed. (Years later she would do the same to my baby daughter, who, unlike me, loved it.) I hated having to sleep with a million sponge rollers attached to my scalp, but so long as I had nice hair for school, my mom was happy, so that was that. When I was in fifth grade, my mom started taking me to White Gloves and Party Manners classes, kind of a finishing school for kids where you learn about good hygiene, table manners, phone etiquette, and so on. Underneath the Southern curls and the lace dresses, I was a goofy tomboy, but I learned at a young age where to place a napkin on the table, in what order the forks, spoons, and knives went, how to correctly get in and out of a car, even how to walk a catwalk—"the essentials of being a true and proper lady," my mother said. "We may be broke, but we don't need to act like it," she said. The older I got, the more I rebelled against all that. I would do everything in my power *not* to look perfect—to scuff my shoes and dirty my cheeks. I broke the rules because the reality behind our white picket fence didn't match the façade.

Now, I *loved* my daddy, Bobby Brown. But truth be told, he was an angry motherfucker. My mom always tried to shield me from it, but it was obvious that Bobby had some ugly rage that festered deep inside. I must have been five years old the first time I decided to step in. Bobby was getting Judy really bad, kicking her on the floor. So I grabbed a bottle of ketchup, lay down, and squirted the red stuff all over my belly, so as to create a diversion.

"Look over here, Daddy, I'm hurt. You must get help."

Bobby cocked his head to one side. "You better get out of here, Bobbie," he growled. "Yes, get out!" my mom screamed. I wasn't sure who was more mad at me, my dad or my mom. She really hated my seeing her like that.

Judy tried to leave Bobby numerous times. She would pack a few suitcases and we would go stay at a hotel, but my dad would show up looking all lonesome and sorry for himself and convince us to come home. He just had this way with words, the ability to make you fall in love with him all over again, no matter what he had just done. Things would get good for a while, and our little house on Pioneer Drive would be filled with music. My daddy played the guitar, mandolin, and harmonica; once upon a time, he even had dreams of being a country singer. A lot of blues and country singers came from his hometown of Spartanburg—Pink Anderson (inspiration for the Pink in Pink Floyd), David Ball, and Walter Hyatt, for instance. When I was little, I would sit up with him late and listen to him strum on his guitar. Those were my favorite times with him. Sometimes my dad would perform in a little bar close to where we lived. When he wasn't performing at the bar, he'd be drinking it dry.

Bobby didn't drink much at home, but he loved to go out and party, and when he came stumbling onto the front porch, that's when the fun and games began. I could hear them in their bedroom, my mom yelling at him to stop. After a while Mom would have me sleep in bed with her, hoping perhaps that I could act as a safety barrier. But it didn't work. Bobby Brown couldn't help himself—a trait that ran in his family.

"Bobbie, honey, wake up."

It was the night of my seventh birthday and I had fallen asleep hours ago, high on cake and soda pop. I opened my eyes and blinked, trying to make sense of what was happening. My mom was leaning over me, stroking my hair.

"Grandpa John just went to heaven; now we gotta take him to the funeral home. You have to get up, sweetie."

Grandpa John was my dad's dad. I was his favorite, the only kid he really liked out of all his children and his children's children. In fact, I may have been the only human being he liked, period. Grandpa John grumbled, growled, and complained, and had beaten up his poor wife, my grandma Ida, like it was his daily duty. A sweet, mild-mannered woman, she had died before I was born, after suffering a brain hemorrhage. My dad was a teenager at the time of her death.

"The heat was on high in the house when I came home," my dad told me, when I was in my twenties. "That's when I knew something was wrong." On a hot Southern day he found my grandma lying on the couch with the heating turned on high. He thought she was sleeping, but she was dead.

My dad remained loyal to my grandpa, though, and when Grandpa John got sick in 1975, he moved in with us. I was six years old and tried my hardest to be a good nurse for him. I would steal pink geraniums and pansies from the neighbor's garden, tie them in a posy, and lay them on his bedside table.

"That's my Pickle," said my grandpa, patting my head, ignoring the neighbor in his yard, hollering about his missing flowers. Grandpa John loved to call me Pickle.

We drove eleven hours to Grandpa's funeral in Spartanburg. That was the first time I had ever seen my dad cry. I cried too. Grandpa John was the only grandpa I ever knew, and I loved him. The last piece of advice Grandpa gave my mom before he died was, "Give him a son." He figured that if my mom bore Bobby a boy, that might help lift his mood. And so when I was eight, my mom gave birth to my brother, John Adam Brown, the sweetest little baby on Earth. As for my dad? Well he stayed grumpy, except maybe a little worse. Now I had a baby to worry about, as well as my mom. Usually when things got bad, I would lift baby John out of his crib (we soon started calling him by his middle name, Adam) and we'd hide in the closet. I'd hold him close to me and sing songs until things got quiet again.

Things worsened when my dad quit being a car salesman and started his home-insulation business. Being around chemicals and fiberglass all day long made him tired and irritable. On top of that, he had trouble figuring out how to make money, hard as he tried. Add a hangover every morning, and you've got one mean, pissed-off son of a bitch. Life with the Browns was never a rose garden.

ELEVEN-YEAR-OLD JOYRIDER

The one thing that always cheered me up, apart from playing with my baby brother, was my girlfriends. I learned early on that when family lets you down, your best friends can pull you back up. My BFF Missy Brown lived down the street. My other best friend was Shannon Parker, who lived next to Missy. Then my two other besties, Jenny Mizel and Kelly Winters, lived within walking distance. We were inseparable, like the Pink Ladies from the movie *Grease*, and we loved nothing more than putting on makeup, gossiping about boys, and making up dances to our favorite pop songs. Jenny and I, especially, were into the dancing. As soon as I could walk, I would groove. I stuffed socks into my mom's bras and boogied with the vacuum cleaner while watching *Soul Train*.

"Look, honey, she really loves that black music," said my dad. To this day, hip-hop is my jam.

I was shy in middle school, but once I started dancing at our school talent shows, that changed. When my mom found out, the stage mom that had resided inside her for so long was finally unleashed.

"Okay, let's do it one more time," my mom would say, as Jenny and I practiced our '80s dance moves. We had picked the song "Funkytown" for the sixth-grade talent show.

"A little more like this, Bobbie! And *smile!*"

Winning the talent shows boosted my confidence even more, and I started singing solo in front of the school. I never had an out-of-the-womb amazing voice like Christina Aguilera, but I knew how to entertain a crowd. I'll never forget my mom's proud face after I sang "Over the Rainbow" in front of the whole school. That moment, I think, is when she realized she had an entertainer on her hands.

Along with my newfound confidence came a growing disregard for the rules. I became convinced that I knew better than most adults—and who could blame me, considering how my parents carried on with each other. Nothing was off-limits, as far as I was concerned, including stealing my mom's car and kidnapping my baby brother. I blame my friend Penny's older sister, who was eighteen. She was like a mentor to Penny and me. She taught us how to French kiss on our hands, how to make a boy think you were ignoring him, how to write a love letter, which lip gloss to wear, the importance of blending eye shadow, how much hair mousse to use, why dry shampoo mattered—the important stuff.

I was eleven years old, and so was Penny. Driving an automobile seemed doable. Penny's sister gave us a pretty thorough lesson in her mom's Thunderbird, and by the end of the day we were confident drivers, our little butts propped up on cushions so we could see over the steering wheel, feet barely reaching the pedals. Driving around the block, then pulling up against the curb and parking was a thrill. I'd never felt so grown-up in my life.

One day I thought it would be fun to take my toddler brother out for a spin. I found my mom's car keys, carried him to the car, and sat him in the passenger seat. We drove about fifteen blocks through the subdivision and then back. It was a glorious morning, and my three-year-old brother seemed perfectly at ease with his eleven-year-old chauffeur. Pulling up to the curb outside my parents' house, I was met by an unwelcome sight—my mom in her bedroom slippers, smudged makeup around her eyes.

"Bobbie are you *driving*?"

I put on the parking brake, just like Penny had showed me, unfastened my seat belt, and got out of the car.

"Yes, I'm an excellent driver."

My mom stormed over to the passenger door, opened it, and lifted Adam gently out of the car, holding him close. "There are going to be some changes around here, mark my words," she said, madder than I'd ever seen her. I got my ass whipped pretty hard that night.

When I was in my mid-teens, and in the ninth grade, my mom finally left Bobby for good. One night she woke me and my brother and we tiptoed out of the house, into a new life. She had been planning it in secret for a long time. Our new home was farther away from my friends, and smaller, a three-bedroom townhome. But I didn't care—I was tired of the nights of driving around the bars looking for my dad. I was tired of lying as flat as I could on the floorboard of the car, trying to make myself disappear. I was tired of my mom having to find him, sometimes with another woman, always drunk.

Bobby had started picking on my little brother, which really riled me. I started purposely provoking my dad, hitting him hard on the back of the head with a comb while he was watching TV, calling him names. I would stand, silent, watching him pick a belt out of the closet, or a switch out of the tree. "I'm going to spank you till you cry," he would tell me. But I never let myself shed a tear. They would well in my eyes, but I never let them fall. When my mom told me she was filing for divorce, I felt relieved. And this time when Bobby tried to win her back, it didn't work.

THE MARVELOUS MR. EARL

Mr. Earl LeSage was everything my father wasn't—soft-spoken, softhearted, and practically a teetotaler. He never raised his voice, and he agreed with absolutely everything my mother said. He had a successful flooring and carpeting business, and had met my mom when he did our floors. She was still married to my dad at the time, and Mr. Earl was married too, but it was clear from day one that he would do anything to help her. Sometimes that meant trying to find my dad a job, just so that he could pay our bills. Mr. Earl was always putting in a good word for Bobby, not because he liked him, but because he hated to see my mom suffer. When Judy finally left Bobby, Mr. Earl was also freshly divorced, and waiting with open arms.

Mr. Earl had grown up poor, but had worked very hard to make his business a success. He was kind and caring, and my mom, after years of fighting and struggling with Bobby, finally started to understand what a truly loving relationship could feel like. She fell madly in love, and even quit wearing high heels, so she wouldn't tower over him (he was shorter than her). They made a handsome couple. Mr. Earl always knew how to dress—he wore snakeskin cowboy boots and belts that matched, with slacks and a nice ironed shirt, and he had a quite collection of cowboy hats. He was a gentle man who loved nature, and his favorite thing in the world, perhaps, apart from my mom, was his garden. Corn, beans, potatoes, turnips—you name it, he grew it. He always grew the plumpest, reddest tomatoes in town, the size of small pumpkins and ten times as sweet.

After my mom married Mr. Earl, she, my brother, and I moved in with him into this big old house on four acres of land just outside Baton Rouge. It was pretty there, although the summers were almost intolerably hot. And there was no escaping the lovebugs. Lovebugs (they're also known as "honeymoon flies," and "kissing bugs,") look like flies that are connected by the tail in pairs, stuck to each other for days after they mate. They would drift in huge, slow clouds in the late summer and if your car ran into one of the swarms, you'd have to clean them off right away; otherwise the acid in their blood could strip your paintwork.

"Love hurts," I would sing, as I hosed down my mom's car for the tenth time that week, spraying off the insect carcasses. At night I would sit on the porch with my brother, plug in one of those ultraviolet bug zappers, and listen to the sharp buzz the lamp made as it fried the lovebugs pair by pair. I daydreamed about what summers might be like in other places, places that weren't hot and sticky and full of dead bugs. Places like Los Angeles, with its swaying palm trees, beaches, and rock music.

I had heard that Tommy Lee lived in L.A. This is pertinent because when I was fifteen, Tommy Lee was my absolute number one crush, and my entire bedroom was covered in Mötley Crüe posters. I loved to watch their videos on MTV, and I thought they were *way* cool for wearing makeup. *When I do it for the first time, it's gonna be with Tommy Lee,* I'd think, staring at Tommy on the wall, his lips pouting, blowing obscene kisses my way. Mr. Earl did not understand my Mötley Crüe fascination one bit. One time, when he drove me, my mom, and my brother to Disney World in Orlando—an eight-hour drive—I insisted on blasting Mötley's *Shout at the Devil* the whole entire way. "But this is the *future*," I yelled, every time Mr. Earl tried to turn the music down.

HIGH SCHOOL BOY BLUES

I had made a new friend over the summer, Deanna. We were going to start high school together and I hoped she and I could become best friends. Unbeknownst to me, Deanna had a huge crush on a boy called Mark DuVall. Mark was a year older than us and very handsome. He had invited me to go to the movies a few times, and I was hoping that once we started high school, he might ask me to be his girlfriend. I had mentioned this to Deanna. She smiled, but I guess she wasn't happy about it.

"Hey, you wanna try my mom's tanning bed? It'll make you

look like you've been playing beach volleyball all summer," she said. I had never used a tanning bed before. Twenty-five minutes later, I emerged from the coffin-like bed. My skin felt crispy, brittle.

"You look amazing!" said Deanna, smirking.

A few days later I enrolled at Starkey Academy, a private high school in East Baton Rouge County, with burns all over my face. I was covered in hundreds of tiny painful blisters, swollen and oozing and red as Mr. Earl's tomatoes. Even talking hurt.

"What setting did Deanna have the tanning bed on?" asked my mom, shaking her head as she dabbed chamomile lotion onto my face that morning. "Doesn't she know you have Irish blood?"

"I look cremated," I sobbed.

My mom's rule was that unless you were puking or bleeding, you weren't missing school. Having an incinerated face didn't count, so I had to walk the halls looking like a burn victim for days, until the blisters went away. Then my skin started peeling, and I just looked like a leper. I was too embarrassed to even talk to Mark DuVall, who assumed I didn't like him anymore, and started dating Deanna. With that, the penny dropped. Some girls, I realized, will stop at nothing to get what they want. My very first lesson in love.

Chapter Three

TEENAGE WASTELAND

"Just stay there—*don't move.*"

I had Dirk Arnold pinned to the backseat of his car. Leather seats squeaked in tandem with the frogs croaking outside as I French-kissed him. Fifteen minutes later, I was done. His entire neck was covered in hickeys. "I want everyone to know that you're mine," I said proudly. Dirk examined himself in the mirror. "Gosh, I wonder what my mom's gonna think," he mumbled.

Something had happened to my personality since my mom divorced my dad, a slow but noticeable blossoming. From being the moody girl who would scuff her shoes on purpose and downplay her looks, I started walking with my head held high, just like the models in the fashion magazines I was starting to collect. These days I listened to my mom, especially when she told me I was pretty. When she showed me how to apply lipstick and how to fix my hair, I listened, rather than pushing her away. My mom, delighted at this newfound closeness with her daughter, loved nothing more than taking me shopping. Finally, bonded by retail, we were on the same page. And I looked good. Really good.

Maybe that's why Dirk, my first boyfriend, didn't mind that I was somewhat of a goofball. We would sit in his car for hours listening to Def Leppard, making out until our lips were shredded and my chin was raw from his stubble. I had started teasing my hair just like the hair metal girls I saw on MTV, wearing tight acid-wash jeans with tears in the butt and off-the-shoulder white T-shirts. I posed for photos with friends, pouting and pretending I was a music video star like Tawny Kitaen.

Dirk's sister was Lacey Arnold. She was the same age as me, and a welcome third wheel in our relationship. We always had the best times together. At night we would sneak out of our folks' houses, driving their mom's car into town, ducking every time we saw a cop. We'd go to underground clubs in Baton Rouge and dance until it was two in the morning, everyone around us high on ecstasy. We didn't even know what ecstasy was at that point—we just loved to dance. Late at night we would sneak back home and crawl into bed, getting up bleary-eyed for school in the morning.

"Hey, Boobless! This seat taken?"

Boys, especially the ones who knew they didn't have a chance, had been calling me Boobless Bobbie for years, thanks to my boyish figure and pancake-flat chest. One morning on the school bus, after a long night of dancing and yet another mean Boobless Bobbie jibe, I blew my top.

"Whatever, cheese dick, I'm going to be a model one day, so I'm *supposed* to have no tits."

I was *obsessed* with models. I spent all my pocket money on fashion magazines, not to read the articles but to look at the girls. I would study their poses and marvel at the symmetry of their faces. They were all tall and skinny like me, with full lips and powerful cheekbones and almond eyes. Maybe looking goofy wasn't such a bad thing after all. My favorite models were Christy Turlington, Stephanie Seymour, and Paulina Porizkova. I liked Paulina the most. She was Czech-American, with piercing blue eyes and fine features, and eventually married Ric Ocasek from the rock band the Cars. I thought hers was the most exotic beauty I had ever seen before. I kept photo albums filled with pages I had torn from magazines featuring Paulina and my favorite models in their high-fashion ad campaigns. My boyfriends never understood it. "I think she looks like a snake," said Dirk, as I pointed out Paulina's latest spread in *Vogue*. "You're prettier," he added, and I didn't get it. I thought blondes were so American pie-ish and boring. I wondered if maybe one day I could dye my hair and look just as sexy and imported as my idol. They just didn't make girls like her in Baton Rouge.

Blond and apple pie as I was, I still wondered if maybe, just maybe, I had a shot at being a model too. I didn't want to be a secretary or a nurse or a teacher, and with my grades, it didn't look like a glittering academic career lay ahead of me. My mom had never gone to college, and there wasn't much pressure for me to succeed scholastically. "Being pretty is what you're best at," my mom said when I asked her if she thought I had a shot at being in the magazines. "If you want to make a living at it, why not? We all have to work with what we've got, Bobbie."

My family never raved about my exceptional good looks, but the consensus was Bobbie Brown's looks were probably her greatest—possibly her only real—asset. And if she didn't want to use her prettiness, well . . . Subway was hiring. They would have loved me just as much either way, and it was comforting, knowing there was no huge pressure on me to succeed. But I didn't see myself making foot-long subs in Baton Rouge for the rest of my life. No way.

My new best friend was Mona, a petite girl with big breasts and four sisters all as pretty as she was. She became an ally in my quest to become pretty enough to be a model. But what were we going to do about that chest of mine? I was still flat as a pancake.

"If you drink Dr Pepper, your tits will grow," she told me.

"Are you sure?" I asked.

"Positive."

I drank so much Dr Pepper that summer my tongue turned brown. Sad to say, my chest refused to blossom. All that sugar, combined with the disappointment, made me testy, to say the least. I tried not to care about having boobs anymore, and now that I knew I wanted to become a model, I sure as hell didn't care about school anymore either.

I became a total brat in the classroom, talking back if I didn't agree with something. What my teachers didn't know was that for me, getting sent to the principal's office was no biggie—the school principal was Mona's father, and he always let me off with a warning and some candy. I was starting to learn that in life, it really is about who you know.

"SPREAD 'EM FOR T-BOY"

T-Boy was probably the cutest boy in all Baton Rouge. He was five foot nine, muscular, and very athletic. He was on the football team and wore a letterman jacket. With his brown hair, brown eyes, and juicy lips, he looked like Taylor Lautner run through a 1980s spin cycle. Meow. One night I was sleeping over at a friend's house when T-Boy and a couple of other popular guys came over. There I was, in the kitchen, raiding the fridge in my pajamas, when T-Boy taps me on the shoulder and whispers in my ear.

"I like you, Bobbie. May I call you sometime?"

I had broken up with Dirk, and this kid was an Adonis. So I gave him my number and soon after, we were official. About six months in, I figured it was time we got down to business.

"We should probably have sex, right?" I said to T-Boy one night at my friend Melissa's house. He looked surprised.

"Okay, if you're sure you're ready?"

My first time was more of a first attempt, because neither of us knew what the hell we were doing. I assumed T-Boy was experienced and would show me the ropes, but actually, he was just as clueless as I was. I didn't even know that you were supposed to open your legs. T-Boy rubbed up and down between my closed thighs for an hour before we called it off due to chafing. After two months of fruitless thigh humping, T-Boy made a suggestion.

"Hey, Bobbie, maybe you should try, you know, spreading them open a little?"

I had no clue what he was talking about.

"Try putting your knees to your chest—they really like that," Mona told me. *Thank God for girlfriends,* I thought.

Next time T-Boy and I got together, I pulled my legs close to my chest like my life depended on it. It hurt like hell at first, but once we got the hang of it, it was game on. I was hypnotized by what our bodies could do together. I started sneaking out at night in my mom's car, driving over to his house to have sex, and then tiptoeing back in at 4 A.M. It didn't occur to me that chasing boys and giving them my all might not be a good idea. All I knew was that with T-Boy, I felt safe, warm, and beautiful. I couldn't let go of the feeling.

One night I was on my way home from T-Boy's when I noticed another car following me. I made turns onto random side streets to see if they would follow, and they did. The car followed me all the way home, picking up speed as I did.

A rapist! I thought, heart pounding as I skidded to a halt outside my house. I ran for the garage, rolling underneath the garage door *Mission: Impossible* style, darting up the stairs quietly as I could. Someone pointed a flashlight through the windows, and I ran into my bedroom and hid underneath the sheets, trembling. The doorbell rang, and I heard my mom pad down the hall.

"Who is it?"

No, Mom, don't open the door, I pleaded in my head, wishing she could hear me.

An undercover cop who lived in our neighborhood had spotted me driving and was wondering what I was doing out so late.

"What on *Earth*, Bobbie!" My mom stormed into my room and turned on the lights. Pulling back the covers, she saw I was fully clothed.

"So Lacey needed me, she has this new boyfriend, and he's, like, abusive," I lied.

"Bullshit," said my mom, who never curses. "I'm calling Lacey's parents."

Of course, Lacey's mom scoffed at my tall tale. I was grounded for a couple of weeks and missed T-Boy so much I cried into my pillow every night.

"Mom, please!"

"Cry me a river, Bobbie Jean Brown, you're as full of it as your father."

T-Boy waited until I was ungrounded, and then it was game on again. We were together for nearly two years, a golden couple, invited to all the coolest parties. All the girls wanted to be my friend, and all the boys wanted to high-five T-Boy. We even talked about the future. I stopped dreaming about leaving Baton

Rouge and moving to L.A. to stalk Tommy Lee. I imagined myself having a bunch of babies with T-Boy and playing with them in Mr. Earl's garden. Didn't sound so bad to me—until Bridgette came along.

Bridgette was a hot cheerleader from another school. She had her eye set on T-Boy from day one, and my friends tried to warn me about her, but I didn't feel threatened in the slightest. T-Boy and I were solid. One night, we were all at a party when Bridgette sidled up next to me and showed me something in the palm of her hand.

"Open your mouth," she said.

"What is it?"

"An M&M."

I don't remember anything past that moment, except that at 3 A.M. I showed up at home covered in mud, my hair drenched with Jack Daniel's. I threw up all night, while back at the party, in front of all our friends, Bridgette was getting it on with T-Boy. When I heard that they had hooked up, it was the worst pain I had ever experienced. T-Boy, who had also been drunk, called the house nonstop, apologizing, begging for me to get back with him, but I couldn't. I didn't believe in cheating. "You're nothing but a fake and a loser!" I screamed at him. Heartbroken, I stopped thinking about my future with T-Boy. I reverted to Plan A—get the hell out of Baton Rouge and make my living as a model, preferably a model married to Tommy Lee or some other cute rocker. The pageant circuit was as good a place as any to start.

PAGEANT PRINCESS

In my senior year, I entered the Miss Louisiana Teen USA pageant. My friend Shannon Parker had been doing pageants for years, so I figured I'd tag along. I picked out a long green ball dress, my mom did my hair and makeup, and I lined up along with all the other girls. I went into the contest assuming I had little to no chance of winning. Which didn't bother me too much, as I had been trained by my family not to be too competitive. I couldn't believe the cutthroat, crazy drive that all the other pageant girls had. *If I do good, great, and if I don't, okay,* I thought. Because my goal was never to be the winner, I was able to relax and have fun at the competition.

"So, Bobbie, what's your favorite hobby?" asked one of the judges.

"Well, I probably shouldn't say this, but I love listening to Mötley Crüe and drinking Dr Pepper, primarily for its health benefits."

The audience clapped and roared, entertained by my tomfoolery. In between rounds, the very effeminate gentleman who was directing the pageant pulled me and my mom to one side.

"Mrs. LeSage, I love your girl Bobbie, but that dress—it's *killing* me," he whispered.

I glanced down at my heavy, dark green frock that, truth be told, did have a certain Wednesday Addams feel. Luckily, my mom had thought to bring a backup, a sequined puffy-sleeved prom dress that had a plunging neckline and clung to my body in all the right places. The pageant director beamed when I emerged from the dressing room.

"Bravo, Bobbie, you look just like Krystle Carrington."

When I stepped back onstage, everyone gasped, especially Shannon Parker, who could not believe what she was about to see—Boobless Bobbie Brown winning the very first beauty pageant she had ever entered. I blinked in surprise as they handed me the trophy and named me Miss Louisiana Teen USA, 1987. At just seventeen, I was a real-life beauty queen—and I hadn't even had to try very hard.

Winning the competition was half blessing, half curse. It made me realize I might actually have a shot as a model, a shot at being *somebody*. The kind of girl who deserved a real Prince Charming, one who didn't cheat like T-Boy, and wasn't mean and drunk, like my dad. But the downside of being declared the prettiest girl in Louisiana is that all of a sudden, people start treating you differently. I wasn't mentally prepared for it, because in reality, I didn't actually believe I was the prettiest girl in Louisiana. I couldn't believe how seriously everyone else was taking it. It was just a little local competition, after all! But the girls who I'd thought were my friends started whispering all kinds of things about me behind my back. And the guys—well if they weren't humping on my leg, they were running from me like they were scared. Worst of all, Mona, Shannon, Lacey—my best girlfriends—thought I was getting too big for my boots and froze me out. That was one long, lonely winter, I can tell you.

I tried not to let things get me down, even though I still had trouble comprehending why everyone was making such a fuss about me winning. I had the big competition ahead of me at the end of the summer—Miss Teen USA. I wondered how everyone would treat me after that, and reminded myself that it didn't really matter if I won. All that mattered was getting *some* kind of modeling contract so I could at least leave Baton Rouge, find my rock star, and live a fun and glamorous life like Paulina.

TEEN QUEEN

My mother was always encouraging, always supportive, and took great care of me. From grooming to trips to the dentist to dance class, she was always on top of things. As soon as I was old enough, she took me to get my first Pap smear. To our horror, the results came back positive—abnormal cells indicated that I had early-stage cervical cancer. "You're very lucky we caught it so early," said the doctors. They said they would need to operate to cut out the cancer, and ended up removing half of my cervix. They said that I would probably never be able to have children as a result of the surgery. When I returned from the hospital, my mother and I cried together. She told me that it didn't matter what the doctors said; only God could decide if I was supposed to have babies or not.

"Should I still go to Miss Teen USA?" I asked my mom, holding back the tears.

"Most definitely," she said. "The show must go on."

Come July, me and my momma said hello to the big West Texas moon that shone bright over El Paso the night of the biggest teen pageant in America. The competition was as fierce as the July heat: fifty-one girls from all over the U.S., between the ages of thirteen and nineteen, all competing for the title of Miss Teen USA. I made friends with Kristi Lynn Addis, Miss Mississippi, and she was a doll. We helped zip up each other's dresses for the evening gown competition, and tucked in each other's bathing suit labels. Backstage, we gave each other good-luck hugs before lining up for the big show, which was being televised live across the United States. Our gowns ranged from pouffy to pouffier to pouffiest (this was 1987, after all, the year style forgot), and the El Paso Youth Symphony Orchestra played a classical rendition of Billy Joel's "Uptown Girl" as we prepared to step on the stage.

Bobbie is five foot eight inches tall and weighs one hundred seventeen pounds, said the announcer.

I strutted across the stage, a prom night explosion in salmon pink, shoulder puffs so big you could have hidden a small child in each. My hair was sprayed into a formal chignon, my bangs were tall, and my smile was wider than the Rio Grande. I couldn't believe the size of the audience—I'd never seen so many people in one room before.

Then I had to impress the judges with my interview skills. All the girls donned identical skintight acid-wash jeans with sporty jackets. Miss California was up first. She bragged about not having to work to get good grades. Miss North Dakota said she wanted to open boutiques in New York, Paris, and L.A., forgetting that she was talking to a Texan crowd. Then it was my turn.

So, Miss Louisiana, what would you like to be when you grow up?

"Well, I've always wanted to be a successful model, travel, and make the best of my life . . . and if I can't be a professional model and succeed at what I want to do, I have college plans afterward," I lied.

What would you say to a young girl who says she wants to be a model?

"Just to be herself. . . . Enjoy every moment and smile pretty and big."

Do you have an agent yet?

"No. I need one, though." (Laughs from the audience)

What kind of agent are you looking for?

"One that can get me work." (More laughs)

Again, I was just being myself and not trying too hard. And it seemed to work. The judges named me second runner-up and gave my buddy Kristi from Mississippi the Miss Teen USA crown. I couldn't have been happier. Just knowing I had made the top five was faith-affirming enough to keep me giggling all the way to the airport. When my mom and I boarded that flight back to Baton Rouge, we had no idea what was waiting for us at home—nearly a dozen messages from modeling agencies. Hollywood, apparently, had been watching.

REAL MEN WEAR EYELINER

A few weeks later, my mother and I flew out to Los Angeles to meet some of those prospective agents and managers. The traffic crawled along Sunset Boulevard as kids congregated outside the clubs: the Rainbow, Gazzarri's, the Roxy, the Whisky. It was like a big glam rock street party, guys with guitar cases and leather jackets strolling up and down between the big clubs, while girls who looked like strippers handed out fliers. These kids weren't hippies, and they weren't greasers—they were something new, like magnificently plumed birds in skintight pants, tiger print, spandex, and red leather. My heart pounded as I gazed at all these guys, each one the spitting image of Vince Neil, Axl Rose, or (swoon) Tommy Lee. My mom, naturally, was horrified. "I mean, what kind of man goes out wearing makeup?" she tutted when we got back to our hotel. "Mom, that's the whole point—if you're a real man, you can wear eyeliner and get away with it." But she seemed far less enamored with Hollywood than I.

"Honey, are you *sure* you want to move here?" she asked. I felt sure that I did. Hollywood was where I could really live the life of a model. Not Baton Rouge. "I'll be okay, Mom, I promise. I'm tough, remember?" My mom nodded, and we signed with an agency called East West later the next day. I couldn't wait to get started, but my mom said I had to finish high school first. So back we went to Baton Rouge, which, compared to Hollywood, felt downright quaint now.

I got a job at Body Masters, a new gym Mr. Earl opened

with my mom's brothers Jimmy and Wayne. It was while working reception there that I met Kenny, a rich kid who, like me, had dreams of escaping Baton Rouge. He sang in a rock band and had a long mullet and a mustache. When I told him I was going to move to Los Angeles, his eyes lit up beneath his frizzy bangs.

"Let's go together, Bobbie," he said. "I'll be a rock star, and you can be my super-hot girlfriend." I was nineteen, he was twenty-six, and we were definitely on the same page. A few months later we hit the road with a carful of clothes, headed west toward Sunset.

Chapter Four

SEARCHING FOR A STAR

"Well, don't you look pretty," said O. J. Simpson, standing next to me at the bar, sizing me up like I was the evening's special. Maybe it had something to do with the tight black-and-white minidress I was wearing, but the men were swarming me like flies on shit—Eddie Murphy had introduced himself not five minutes ago, Scott Baio was staring at my ass like it was his long-lost puppy, and now this guy. He looked vaguely familiar.

"Thank you so much," I said, flashing my biggest Southern smile before heading back to the dance floor, a triple vodka cocktail in each hand. One was for me, and the other was for my guy, Kenny. I looked around trying to find him. We were at Helena's, a private supper club in Hollywood, whose members included Jack Nicholson and Madonna. It was an intimate mingle zone for the rich, famous, and beautiful. Being neither rich, nor famous, nor beautiful, Kenny always felt insecure when I brought him to Helena's. I figured triple shots would help.

"Here, babe, drink up!"

"Did you just give O. J. Simpson your phone number,

Bobbie?" asked Kenny, snatching his glass from me, his eyes despondent.

"That was *O. J. Simpson?*" I said, glancing back at the bar. "Well, I'll be damned."

Since arriving in Los Angeles, everything had felt effortless. Hollywood values youth and beauty above all—as a young model with a contract, I was automatically on the list at every hot club in town; the bookers at my agency just told me where to go and who to ask for at the door. Within days, I was cutting lines and breezing through velvet ropes without a thought. It was just part of the job, I figured. Those left waiting in line eyed me jealously. I had no idea how success-driven people are in Los Angeles. I had never had to work for my own, so I took it for granted from day one. Things were not working out as well for Kenny, though. Neither of us could understand why this town wasn't falling in love with him the way it was with me. We had arrived only a few weeks ago, but already I was something of a scene queen. I had enlisted a group of super-babeish girlfriends from the modeling agency, and together we ruled the roost at Helena's, with Kenny tagging along, letting me pay for his drinks at the bar.

Later that night, the R & B singer Bobby Brown came dancing up to me. "Hey, Bobbie Brown, you wanna dance with Bobby Brown?" he said. We danced for a while, and he seemed interested in continuing the conversation, but I politely took my leave. I had arrived with Kenny, and I would leave with Kenny. Maybe it was something they taught me at White Gloves and

Party Manners class in New Orleans—but I simply abhorred cheating. Nobody ever said a little flirting wasn't allowed, but I wasn't about to go around giving out my number.

Helena's was owned by 1970s cult actress Helena Kallianiotes, known for playing a butch lesbian hitchhiker opposite Jack Nicholson in the movie *Five Easy Pieces* and an aggressive Roller Derby girl in *Kansas City Bomber*. Her supper club was a Hollywood fantasyland—not that you'd know from the exterior, until the Ferraris and Rolls-Royces would start lining up at around 10 P.M. Madonna and her then husband, Sean Penn, would be served dinner under a canopy by waiters dressed all in white. Susan Sarandon and Cher would make conversation with Rob Lowe and other Brat Packers. I danced with Judd Nelson, smoked cigars with Harry Dean Stanton, shared lipstick with Melanie Griffith, and talked poetry with her husband, Don Johnson. (I had been writing poems for years, so we shared that in common.) I fit so easily into the scene at Helena's, it was hard for me to remember my "other" life, as a small-time pageant queen in Baton Rouge. My unself-conscious flair for conversation and my relaxed energy made me stand out from the crowd of insecure, overambitious model-actress-whatevers. Having been schooled in Southern manners and etiquette so early in life, I knew how to charm the socks off anyone I was introduced to.

Not once did I stop to think about just how remarkable it was that I, Bobbie Jean Brown, should have so quickly and easily gained access to the most exclusive echelons of the Hollywood scene. In my mind, I was exactly where I was supposed to be.

My don't-give-a-fuck attitude was serving me well. I'd march up to the front of every line as though it was my God-given right, look the bouncer in the eye, and wink, with the confidence of a star who had already made it. And they would let me in, not because I was necessarily more beautiful than anyone else in line (L.A. is chock-full of beauty), but because of my fearlessness. Of course, this is only the kind of game that you can get away with for so long. Unless you back up the bullshit with some bona fide success, sooner or later, Hollywood will tire of the façade and swiftly, brutally put you back in your place.

Hollywood was bored with Kenny almost the second he arrived in town. He had very little charm behind those good looks, and absolutely nothing in common with Don Johnson, Melanie Griffith, or anyone else at Helena's. He was out of his league, and no matter how many triple vodkas I brought him, it seemed like nothing could pull him out of his funk.

We were sharing a one-bedroom apartment on Riverside Drive in North Hollywood, in the sprawling superheated basin known as the San Fernando Valley, home to gum-snapping Valley girls, salon tanners, and porn stars. It was close enough to the action for me, just a ten-minute drive into the land known as "Hollywood," encompassing the music venues and nightclubs of the Sunset Strip, the bars of West Hollywood, and the glitzy restaurants and hotels of Beverly Hills.

Los Angeles rewards youth, beauty, and balls—all of which I possessed by the boatload—so I started booking jobs almost the minute we arrived. These included my very first music video, for the song "I'm On to You" by a semipopular heavy metal band called Hurricane. "I'm On to You" was the only Top 40 hit Hurricane ever had, and when I found out, I shrugged, thinking, *Of course.* Everything I touched turned to gold. I was a young model in Hollywood, making friends, making money, and starting to hang out with rock stars. Everything was going according to plan. I couldn't believe just how *easy* it was.

Look closely at that video, and you'll notice my nose has a little bump in it. Also, my chest is nothing to write home about. But about two weeks after the shoot, my face and body had taken on new dimensions, thanks to a very nice plastic surgeon, whose services were paid for by my mom. I loved my brand-new D cups, but I knew there was no way I was ever going to be the next Cindy Crawford or Christie Brinkley. First, I was too short to be a supermodel, and now my figure was far too juicy for high fashion. I was sexy in a California surfer–girl next door kind of way, not a pinched New York runway model way. And I was okay with that. The L.A. look was hot, and it was *so* me—blond, bubbly, and rock 'n' roll. This was the era of casual sporty chic, of L.A.-centric TV shows like *Beverly Hills 90210* and *Melrose Place*, and the poppy hair metal music exploding out of Hollywood was the hottest thing on the *Billboard* charts. I recalibrated my high-fashion aspirations and rebranded myself as the ultimate California babe, switching to a different agency, Flame, which specialized in a mainstream, commercial look. The gamble paid off—at Flame I found myself busier than before, with photo shoots, auditions, and test shoots, not to mention more music videos. To me, they were just another money gig, as workaday as a Sears catalog shoot. I never thought any of those shoots would make or break my career.

The second video I did was with a short-lived pop duo, Times Two, who were touring the country as Debbie Gibson's opening act. I wore a tasseled black outfit and go-go danced in the video to their 1989 pop take on Simon & Garfunkel's "Cecilia." I'm ashamed to say, I had never even heard of Simon & Garfunkel. Or Times Two (which is more forgivable). Then the rock band Great White called, saying they wanted me for the video for "Once Bitten Twice Shy," a cover of Ian Hunter's (Mott the Hoople) original. It was a fun shoot. I got to play a hot groupie babe, sitting on the back of lead singer Jack Russell's Harley, looking babeish with a bunch of other groupie babes while wearing a leather bra with studs. The song would become the band's biggest hit, charting at number 5 on the *Billboard* Hot 100, earning them a Grammy nomination for Best Hard Rock Performance and some sell-out tours with Bon Jovi. *But of course*, I thought.

When Great White, now bona fide rock stars, called me back for a second video shoot for "House of Broken Love," my job was to wear blue jeans and a white T-shirt, stand on a desert highway, and look lonesome. The shoot was less fun than the "Once Bitten" shoot—Jack Russell, the lead singer with a pair of lungs that rivaled Robert Plant's, was starting to use drugs again and was having difficulty leaving his trailer. Nonetheless, the song was a hit, and gained me a little recognition, especially when they used my photo for the cover of the single.

Not long afterward, I shot the "Sittin' in the Lap of Luxury" video with Louie Louie, who had played Madonna's boyfriend in the video for "Borderline." I could see why Madonna had chosen him for the job; he was one of the sexiest guys I had ever met, but as sweet as he was, he showed absolutely zero interest in me ☹. Terence Trent D'Arby, on the other hand, was nothing *but* friendly when I was hired to dance in the video for his "It Feels So Good to Love Someone Like You." He had apparently told the press that his debut record was "better than [the Beatles'] *Sgt. Pepper*." A few years later his career tanked, so he changed his name to Sananda Maitreya and moved to Italy. Hollywood is a cruel mistress.

SOUTHERN FRIED

Kenny, having grown up rich and spoiled in Baton Rouge, had no work ethic whatsoever. He thought he could just show up in L.A. with his curly mullet and mustache and land a record deal straightaway. But guys like him were a dime a dozen. They waited tables and washed cars, hustling while trying to get a foot in the door. Kenny had no foot *close* to any door, so he just terrorized me instead.

"Did you fuck that French fuck?" he screamed at me one evening. I had just stepped in the door, home from a test shoot that day with a fabulous European photographer. I threw the black-and-white photos angrily on the kitchen table, too frustrated to even argue. He was pressuring me to quit modeling, give up the dream. I was starting to think he was losing his mind. The next day, he did.

I stopped at the bank on my way home, and was politely informed that both my accounts had been completely drained by the other joint account holder, Kenny, just that morning. *Now why would he do a thing like that?* I wondered, rushing home from Wells Fargo. I opened the front door to our apartment, and Kenny was sitting on the floor, cutting up photos of me with my sewing scissors, shredding my face into thousands of little pieces. My whole portfolio, gone; my bank accounts, drained. Kenny was having a fucking meltdown. I had no idea how to handle it.

My best friend at the time was a model-actress-dancer called Rebecca Ferratti, a *Playboy* Playmate in 1986, and star of many a hair metal video. I locked myself in our bedroom and called her, told her she had to come over with her boyfriend, a tough-looking Italian actor called Jimmy Franzo.

"Yo, Kenny! It's Jimmy. Open the fucking door!"

I was hiding in the closet but could hear everything that was happening; Kenny was sobbing as he let Jimmy in.

"Kenny, bro, you gotta go. C'mon, pack some shit, I'll take you to the airport."

Jimmy drove Kenny straight to LAX and put him on a plane back to Louisiana that night. When I called Mr. Earl and told him what had happened, he sent one of my uncles over to Kenny's house to gently—so very gently—request that Kenny pay Miss Bobbie Jean Brown the five thousand dollars she had been so generous as to loan him from her bank account.

SCOTT BAIO BUMMER ZONE

I was happy that Kenny, with his jealous mood swings and shitty attitude, was out of my life. I was single and ready to mingle. One of the first dates I went on was with Scott Baio, who I had met at Helena's. I remembered him as Chachi, the cute guy in that show *Happy Days*. I was a little surprised when he invited a buddy to dinner with us, a chirpy little yes-man who loved to chime in and agree with whatever Scott had to say. *Maybe that's just the Hollywood way,* I thought.

"Hollywood is a dark, twisted place, Bobbie," said Scott, with a faraway look in his eyes.

"Yeah," said his friend.

"Something about it here just brings out the worst in us all," continued Scott, toying with his fettuccini.

"You'll see," added his friend.

Jeez Louise. What a pair of depressives! After having to put up with Kenny and his bummer vibes, this was the last thing I needed. I had only just arrived in town and was having my Hollywood honeymoon. Little did I know that, as Scott Baio warned, the city will start playing tricks on your mind if you let it. But that night, I just thought Scott was a negative Nancy. Also he had these thin little lips, and my mom always said never to trust a man with thin lips. When those thin lips headed toward mine at the end of the date, I made a side dodge and air-kissed Scott on the cheek. He smiled, surprised. "See you around, Bobbie," he said, and I nodded, sure that he would.

BREAKING THE CHIPPENDALES CODE

A few nights later, I found myself in the middle of a throng of screaming women in downtown L.A. It was mass hysteria at the Chippendales show.

"Take them off!" screamed the woman next to me, and I had to put my hands over my ears. Women were standing on tables, hanging off railings, desperately reaching out for the sweaty hunks in G-strings, hungry for man flesh. It was like feeding time at the zoo.

My girlfriend had dragged me along, promising a good time. I wasn't so sure, until my eyes came to rest on one of the dancers. He had long hair and tattoos, and looked like a Viking warrior.

"You can get us backstage, right?" I yelled at my girlfriend, who rolled her eyes.

"Duh!" she said. "Of course!"

The dangerous stud with the Viking physique was named Mike. My skin stuck to his as we kissed later that night in his dressing room, his body still covered in oil. I could feel the stubble on his chest as I ran my hands over his solid pectorals. What a hottie.

The following weekend, we went back to the Chippendales show, and again the following week. Each time, Mike and I would meet up afterward and fuck; in the bathroom, in the parking lot, wherever we could snatch a few moments alone. Each time ended with a smile and a "see you soon," but Mike never did ask me for my number.

Maybe it's the Chippendales code of honor, I thought. *Perhaps they are banned from dating the audience.*

One day I was driving through Hollywood, and there he was, Mr. Mike Chippendale, standing in a hotel parking lot.

"Hey there!" I yelled from the window of my red Honda.

He saw me and looked surprised.

"Well, hello there, beautiful."

It was nice seeing Mike in the daylight. He seemed different somehow. I invited him over to my place later, and not long after he walked in the door, we were kissing.

"I never even noticed your dimples before," I said, touching Mike's cheek.

"You're so beautiful, Bobbie," he said, kissing me tenderly. He came over the next night, and the night after that. I was falling in love.

"I can't believe I'm dating a Chippendale!" I told my girlfriend on the phone. I had been seeing Mike for nearly a month.

"Well, let's go visit your new stripper boyfriend, shall we?" she said.

I got all dressed up. Sexy was in fashion, and my skirt was short and skintight; my sheer flesh-toned blouse had a neckline that plunged deep. I sat way in the back, my eyes fixed on Mike. His onstage character and his real-life self were so different, I thought, applauding wildly. Afterward, I snuck backstage and leapt on top of Mike as soon as I saw him.

"Whoa, girl, this is a surprise," he said, glancing around nervously. "Thanks for coming."

"You're so amazing," I said, kissing him. "So I was thinking, you know, maybe you should move in."

"Move in where?"

"My place, silly."

"Where's your place?"

It was hard to tell who was more spooked. A few minutes of Q&A later, we got to the bottom of the mystery—as it turned out, the Mike who I had been fucking for the last month was not the Mike standing in front of me. The Mike standing in front of me had a twin brother called Steve, and apparently this wasn't the first time Steve had pretended to be his brother. Mike swore he had no idea that Steve had been deceiving me for the last month.

"I'm sorry I never asked for your number, Bobbie, it's just that I have a girlfriend," said Mike. "Also, I'm sorry about Steve—he's an asshole."

I called Steve as soon as I got home, in tears. Fifteen minutes later, he was outside my front door, pleading with me to let him in.

"You're an asshole, Mike—I mean, Steve, or whoever you are," I yelled.

The neighbors were peering out their front doors, wondering what new romantic disaster was taking place at Bobbie's.

"I'm sorry, Bobbie, I was going to tell you. . . ."

"The truth happens to be something I'm fond of, asshole! I already told you how much I hate liars."

It took Steve about two hours to smooth-talk his way back into my arms. I kind of preferred Steve to Mike anyway. So I let him move in. Dumb move.

"Do you want to get high?" he said one night, a few months after he became my live-in guy. He was holding a little bag of cocaine. I had tried ecstasy a couple of times, but never coke. *What's the harm?* I figured, watching him cut two big lines the color of dirty snow. Upon inhaling, I noticed the acrid chemical taste in my throat—"nose candy" was a misnomer, because this tasted like shit. But Steve and I made love for hours that night. I told him everything; about Kenny, about my dad, about Mr. Earl. I hadn't opened up to anyone this much since leaving Baton Rouge.

Unlike Kenny, Steve loved going out with me to all the clubs and could hold his own. But he too found it hard to control his jealousy, especially when famous guys showed an interest in me. Like Prince, for example.

"Prince would love to meet you; care to follow me to his table?"

I was at Prince's new club in downtown L.A., called Vertigo. It was the city's first "New York–style" club, meaning it didn't matter how much money you had, you had to look good in order to get in. Movie stars, beautiful people, and exotic-looking club kids would bounce between there and Helena's on a typical Friday night. The scene outside was frantic, huge bouncers in Armani suits and headsets, and a door run by Studio 54's former gatekeeper, Marc Benecke. Inside, the most glamorous people in the world mingled on a dance floor built by Mary Pickford and Rudolph Valentino. The Brat Packers were there, Emilio Estevez and Matt Dillon, and Princess Stéphanie of Monaco. And of course Prince and his protégée Vanity.

He had sent one of his assistants over to say hello. My jaw dropped—*me*? I *love* Prince. *Purple Rain* is one of my all-time favorite albums. Steve looked at me with murderous eyes.

"She's busy," he growled to Prince's assistant, grabbing me by the arm and pulling me away. Prince's assistant shook his head and walked away. Moments later, Rob Pilatus, the handsome singer from Milli Vanilli, started dancing with me. I felt Steve's hand on my shoulder again.

"That's it, we're leaving," he said, handing me my coat.

"Good-bye," said Rob, in his thick German accent, shrugging.

After six months living with Steve, I found myself wondering if it was Steve I was in love with, or the cocaine. I was spending all my modeling money on blow. I was missing jobs and spacing out on appointments because I had the cocaine blues. I would get high in bathroom stalls at shopping malls, buy shoes fueled by the rush, and then forget where I parked my car. Already slim, I started dropping holes on my belt as the weight fell off, because I was too high to eat. I was not a high-functioning addict and never would be. Although at that point, I would never have referred to myself as an addict. I just liked to party; so did everyone in L.A.

One night, I came home from a late shoot to find that Steve had brought home a surprise.

"Bobbie, meet Brandi. She's a lesbian."

Steve was always pulling weird shit on me, but this was a first. I lacked the energy and the wherewithal to argue with Steve and his simmering libido.

"Okay," I said, stretching out my hand. "Pleasure to meet you." I had seen her out and about at the clubs. When Steve and Brandi started kissing, I really wasn't sure what to do with myself.

"Here," said Steve, throwing a bag of coke on the table. Brandi's eyes were on me. I felt Brandi's hands massage my shoulders as I cut some lines and inhaled the powder. Her bare breasts were dangling above the back of my head, and I noticed her nipples were pierced.

Oh.

Brandi pulled me down on the carpet and slipped her hand up my miniskirt, pulling it far enough to reveal my panties. Steve watched. I had never been with a woman before. Her skin smelled of cinnamon and tobacco. She pulled my panties to one side and started going down on me. After about two seconds I jumped up. "I just gotta go do something, I'll be right back!" It was all too much for me to take in. I left the room and waited a few minutes, expecting Steve to follow me. When he didn't, I peeked back into the living room, and Steve was feverishly fucking Brandi from behind. He climaxed with a mighty groan, and Brandi turned around, horrified.

"You came inside me, asshole!" she said. "I told you not to."

They had made a deal that he could fuck her in return for access to me, so long as he promised to pull out before he came. Steve, as we were all starting to realize, was not one to keep his word.

Two months later, Brandi came over. She was pregnant with Steve's baby, apparently. Well, that was it for me. "First you're a fake Chippendale, and now you're having a baby with a lesbian?" I screamed.

I got out of that apartment in North Hollywood, moving in with a fellow model called Shantae in Hollywood proper. Together, we decreed our home a loser-free zone. And absolutely no Chippendales—fake or otherwise—allowed. My days of dating down were over.

BEDTIME STORIES WITH NELSON

In 1990, I met golden-haired rock star Matthew Nelson on the set of *Star Search*, an *American Idol*–style televised talent show that was hugely popular. Competitors sang, danced, joked, and modeled for a top prize of $100,000. My agency had sent me along to compete in the "spokesmodel" category, and the setup was so similar to pageantry, it was easy. Winning *Star Search* is a tried and tested path to the big time—the singer Aaliyah had won the year before; Christina Aguilera would win that year; and Beyoncé and Justin Timberlake would be champions a few years later. I got off to a great start—every week I competed, I won. I found myself on one of the longest winning streaks in the show's history, and millions were tuning in just to see if Bobbie Jean Brown was going to win the modeling competition again. For the first time in my life, I started realizing that maybe, just maybe, I was actually beautiful. Not just cute, not just adorable, not just entertaining . . . but beautiful. Admitting that to myself made me feel uneasy. Because with beauty comes power, and with power comes responsibility. I had never thought beyond just getting to L.A. and making a few bucks and finding a rocker boy. In no way was I mentally prepared for the opportunities that my beauty was generating—in just a year, my small- to medium-size ambition had already gotten me much farther up the ladder than girls who spend their whole twenties in Hollywood. All I knew was that I was getting more and more famous, and getting more and more attention from men. Deep down, I longed for someone—my guitar-wielding Prince Charming—to just whisk me away from it all and promise to take care of me forever.

Matthew Nelson was friends with the wardrobe person on the show, and he came to visit the set with his twin brother, Gunnar. They were Hollywood brats, the twin sons of Rick Nelson, one of the biggest teen idols of the 1950s and America's top-selling singer—bar Elvis—between 1957 and 1962. Rick

Nelson's songs were among the first rock 'n' roll tunes to be embraced by the mainstream—thanks to his parents and their family-friendly TV show, *The Adventures of Ozzie and Harriet*. Matthew and Gunnar figured they had inherited some of their dad's talent and had formed a band called Nelson, playing a radio-friendly blend of hair metal and easy listening that was especially popular among teenage girls. Their 1990 debut album, *After the Rain*, would sell more than a million copies, and onstage, they were matching Rapunzels who rocked, with Matthew on bass and Gunnar on lead guitar, blond hair cascading like golden showers.

What is it with me and identical twins? I thought, smiling sweetly as they introduced themselves in my dressing room. Gunnar was the louder, more obnoxious of the brothers, and Matthew was a little more reserved. When Matthew shyly asked me for my phone number, I said yes. He wasn't like the other hair rock guys, hanging out with porn stars and strippers, burying his face in pussy and blow every night. Matthew did not touch drugs or alcohol of any kind, and neither did Gunnar. They had seen what alcoholism had done to their father.

In his later years, Rick Nelson had become a heavy substance abuser. According to various reports, the death of his father, Ozzie, as well as his unhappy marriage to Gunnar and Matthew's mom, Kris, had pushed Ricky to spend two to three hundred days a year on the road, pill-popping and partying his way around the nation. Ricky was killed on New Year's Eve 1985 in an airplane accident over De Kalb, Texas, with cocaine, marijuana, and the painkiller Darvon in his bloodstream. Having a father who became a cautionary tale deeply impacted the brothers, and they prided themselves in their sobriety.

GOOD TWIN, BAD TWIN

Matthew was the perfect gentleman I had been looking for—perfect, that is, except for his evil twin. Gunnar seemed threatened by me. Maybe it was because his brother was so devoted to me. Gunnar's Beverly Hills girlfriend Laurel also behaved like an asshole toward me, in a sort of passive-aggressive way. For instance, she and Gunnar would often discuss their sex life in intimate detail in front of me, knowing that it made me uncomfortable.

Ew, I thought, leaving the room.

It didn't help that things had become challenging with Matthew in the bedroom. Matthew always liked me to invent scenarios and fantasies, and describe them at length, otherwise he couldn't get in the mood. I had always been a good storyteller, but Scheherazade I was not, and I found it tiring, having to conjure new sexual narratives night after night. I missed quickies, I missed hard, raw, spontaneous fucking. I wanted it to be more passionate than this.

One night, I was at a Hollywood club called Spice when Rob Pilatus from Milli Vanilli grabbed my hand and led me to the dance floor. I had seen him several times out and about since we first met. But this was the first time we had danced so close to each other. As the beat intensified, I tried yelling something in his ear, but he shook his head.

"My English is very bad!" he said, shaking his head and laughing. "Let's dance now!"

A beautiful man who does not require me to speak. What a relief.

He pulled me close and put his arms around my hips. My buttocks rubbed on his crotch as we moved in the dark. He had model looks, and a break-dancer's moves. For the first time in my life, I'd met someone who rocked the dance floor as hard as I did. When I turned around, his eyes were like emeralds glowing between his long dreadlocks.

"Will you be my girlfriend?" he yelled, over the music.

"Okay," I yelled back. The following day, I told Matthew we were through.

I didn't realize just how troubled Rob really was until we became close. His mother had been a stripper in Germany, and he had spent some of his childhood in orphanages. The pain of his past didn't reveal itself until later—at first, it was nonstop fun, dance floor after dance floor, party after party. His Milli Vanilli bandmate, Fab Morvan, was dating my roommate Shantae, so each night we would return to our place and carry the party on until the sun rose. I loved to see the peachy-pink light of an L.A. dawn, dotted with palm trees in silhouette. There's something magical about it.

Rob and Fab were the toast of Hollywood at the time—their number one hit, "Girl You Know It's True," had just won them the 1990 Grammy for Best New Artist, and the world was in

love with their dance-pop raps and MTV-friendly break dancing. I did think it was a bit odd that not once during our few
months of dating did Rob rehearse or step foot inside a recording studio. And when he sang along to music in the car in his
broken English, it was clear he was tone-deaf. Later, it was
revealed that they were fakes. Neither Fab nor Rob had ever
sung on a Milli Vanilli record—their Machiavellian producer,
Frank Farian, had simply hired them to be the pretty faces of
his consumer product, and the industry lapped it up. When a
coked-up Rob told *Time* magazine that he was the new Elvis,
they printed every word, even though Rob was clearly unable to
differentiate between fantasy and reality. His mood swings were
erratic, he rarely slept, and his hygiene was poor. Very poor.
At the end of the night, he was generally too coked up to have
sex. And on the rare occasions where he was sexual, he usually
liked the attention focused on his ass. This was something new
for me, and it wasn't much fun for me at all. This was not what
I had bargained for. Rob was too strung out. Matthew had been
pursuing me throughout my time with Rob, leaving flowers and
notes on my car, begging me to come back to him. When Rob
left town to go on tour, I decided to give him another chance.

"*Now* will you move in with me, Bobbie?" he asked. He and
Gunnar had recently moved into a charming house in Sherman
Oaks, in the Valley. Matthew and I would take one bedroom,
and Gunnar and Laurel would be in the other. "Okay. But Gunnar better not be a jerk," I said. "Gunnar wants what's best for
me, and he wouldn't dare come in between you and me," said

Matthew, stroking my hand. I think we both knew that was wishful thinking.

A few months after Rob split, the Milli Vanilli fraud would be exposed (by none other than the man who created it, Frank Farian) and the media unleashed a tidal wave of hate upon Rob and Fab. It wasn't fair. They weren't the only lip-synchers to score a hit in the 1990s—C+C Music Factory and Black Box both used uncredited Martha Wash vocals on their top-charting tracks. But Milli Vanilli were the scapegoats, the ultimate lip-synching fake pop stars. Their Grammy was taken away, and Rob and Fab became the laughingstock of pop. Rob, sadly, wasn't strong enough to weather the storm, and in 1998 he died from a drug overdose.

Chapter Five
BIRTH OF A VIDEO VIXEN

Jani Lane, lead singer of the hair metal band Warrant, and his buddy Tommy Lee, drummer for Mötley Crüe, were sitting in a hotel room, watching TV. They were on a sixteen-month tour of America, a wild hair metal extravaganza with Warrant opening for Mötley at sold-out venues across the nation. Warrant were the new kids on the glam metal block, surfing the wave of their number one hit of summer 1989, "Heaven," from their debut album, *Dirty Rotten Filthy Stinking Rich*, which hit number 2 on the Hot 100.

"Wow, she's kind of a babe, huh?" said Jani, nodding at the TV. They were watching *Star Search*, and the babe was me.

"Oh yeah!" said Tommy, rubbing his nose. "*Smokin'*."

As they channel surfed, Tommy swigged from a bottle of Jack Daniel's, elaborating on the different things he planned to do to my body as soon as he got back to L.A. (no matter that he was still very married to TV star Heather Locklear at the time). But Jani, who loved a little friendly competition, claimed first dibs—he had set eyes upon me before Tommy, after all. The two men laid down the challenge: The race was on to see who could bed Bobbie Brown first.

When Jani told me about this bet several years later, I tried to imagine how my fifteen-year-old self might have reacted had she been a fly on the wall. She would no doubt have suffered some kind of a heart attack at the thought of her idol, Tommy Lee, expressing interest in her. Jani Lane, on the other hand, I was less excited by. I had never even heard of Warrant.

Meanwhile, back on the *Star Search* set, I was bawling my eyes out, having just lost out on the $100,000 prize money that everyone in the nation—myself included—had assumed would be mine. I had been on the show for nearly a year, with thirteen consecutive wins in the modeling category, more than anyone in the whole history of the show. I really, *really* wanted to win. Not only would it have been my biggest paycheck ever, it would also be conclusive proof that I, Bobbie Brown, had made it, all by myself. But it wasn't to be. I couldn't help but replay the night's events in my mind, over and over.

I remembered Ed McMahon, the host, onstage holding the $100,000 prize in his hands. I was on one side of him, and Debbie James, the other finalist, was on his other, as the nation held its breath in anticipation of the four judges' decision. Ed opened the envelope and stumbled as he read the winner's name—it wasn't mine. Debbie broke down in victory tears, and I kept my pageant queen smile in place for about two seconds before running offstage. This was the worst night of my life.

I lay on my back on my dressing room floor, ball gowns and

bikinis all over the carpet. I had locked the door and didn't want to talk to anyone. I was too humiliated. Millions of people had just watched me lose on live TV. *This is a major career setback,* I thought. From now on, I would be "that girl who lost *Star Search.*" I thought I was done, washed-up. But I should have remembered from my experience at the Miss Teen USA pageant that sometimes, even when you lose, you win. Because you never do know who's watching.

My agency called, saying the hair band Warrant had been hounding them, wanting to book me for their upcoming video, "Cherry Pie." I was not in the greatest headspace to be auditioning. Despite getting back together with Matthew, the old habits I had revisited with Rob had proven hard to shake off. I was addicted to the dance floor and the coke-fueled lifestyle that was attached to it. Spice and the Roxbury were my glitzy Hollywood haunts; the Cathouse, the Roxy, and the Rainbow were where I rocked out with the hair guys. Increasingly, Matthew was expressing his concerns about my hedonistic lifestyle. He had grown up seeing the lows that inevitably follow the highs of the Hollywood party scene. But I thought Matthew and Gunnar were boring, and their lecturing was driving me to party even more, and it was affecting my career. My manager and agent despaired of my no-shows, my increasing lateness, my flaky attitude. It was no surprise to them when I failed to show for my first meeting with Warrant, but the band's management was relentless. They called again. And again.

"Bobbie, they've got a major hard-on for you," said my

agent. "Can you please just meet with them and get them off my back?"

"Oh, fine, whatever. I'll go."

I was told to meet Jani Lane and his "people" at Jerry's Deli in Sherman Oaks, in one hour. I was, of course, late. Bleary-eyed from partying the night before, I slid into the booth next to Jani, picking a French fry off his plate.

"Thanks," I said, licking my lips. I had a killer hangover. "I'm Bobbie, what's up?"

They told me about the video concept and asked if I'd be okay with wearing little shorts while the band hosed me down.

"Um, sure."

Jani barely said a word. I picked another French fry off his plate.

"So, what's the name of your band again? Torrent?"

"It's Warrant. We just toured with Mötley," said Jani.

"Oh, I fucking *love* Mötley Crüe! So you know Tommy Lee?"

"Of course," said Jani. "You in?" They hired me on the spot, and a few days later I was blasting their song, "Cherry Pie," in my car tape deck on the way to the video shoot. I didn't even know much about the hair scene, to be honest. Apart from Mötley and Def Leppard, I didn't listen to rock. I had always preferred soul, dance, hip-hop, and rap. Bobby Brown, Whitney Houston, Mary J. Blige. New jack swing. When it came to my musical tastes, I had always been the blackest white girl in Baton Rouge, and probably on the Sunset Strip too. But "Cherry

Pie" I liked. It was fun and poppy. It had a cool hook, and I could picture strippers the world over go-go dancing to it.

She's my cherry pie
Put a smile on your face
Ten miles wide

Catchy, I thought. Apparently the head of Columbia Records, Don Ienner, had called Jani asking for a "Love in an Elevator"–type rock anthem, and Jani had come up with "Cherry Pie" in about fifteen minutes, writing the lyrics on a pizza box (the box is now on display at the Hard Rock Cafe in Destin, Florida). At that time, no one had any idea just how much of a hit it would be.

"Hey, Bobbie, you look nice," said Jani, giving me a sideways glance as I walked on set. I peered at him over my sunglasses. He was dressed even more wildly than when we had met at Jerry's. With his teased blond hair and sprayed-on ripped jeans, his image seemed much louder than he was. I hoped he'd relax a little before the "bedroom scene" I'd seen in the treatment. I hadn't told Matthew about that part. He was already upset that I was doing the video in the first place. Nelson was at number 1 with their hit "Love and Affection," but Matthew knew it was all too easy to become last week's news. It seemed disloyal, as far as he was concerned, for me to be starring in a competing band's video.

Hair metal had, at this point, become part of the MTV hit machine. Record labels wanted pretty boys with tight pants and eyeliner to feed the craze for as long as it lasted, one after the next after the next. Hurricane, Autograph, Keel, Vain—the list of one-hit hair metal wonders is endless. Hair metal was never going to be an art form that lasted, it was supposed to be a fireworks show—a shocking, colorful, and short-lived event that burnt itself out less than a decade after it started. By the time Penelope Spheeris's documentary *The Decline of Western Civilization Part II* came out in 1988, capturing the vanity, hubris, and self-importance of the L.A. glam metal scene, kids were already starting to lose respect for it. Anyone who was in a hair band in 1990 was probably starting to feel the futility of it all. For Nelson, Warrant, and all the newer hair bands, there was an unavoidable sense that it was now or never.

In the dressing room, I surveyed the outfits the stylist had laid out for me—skimpy red bustier with tiny denim shorts and red cowboy boots. *Cute.* Roller-girl waitress. Baseball groupie. *Wow, there are a lot of costumes,* I thought. I put on the red bustier and shorts first, walked out onto the set, and stood in front of the guys.

"So?" I asked no one in particular.

"Fucking hot," said Jani.

"So? Bobbie, you see that bathtub over there? You're going to be naked and we're going to fill it with whipped cream."

"Gross. You're out of your mind," I said, walking away.

The second day of shooting, an assistant handed me a bouquet of roses. I glanced at the card, thinking how sweet it was of Matthew to be sending flowers to me on the Warrant set.

For my cherry pie. Love, Jani

Oh. I waved the flowers at Jani, mouthing, "Thanks."

I overheard Jani talking to the director, saying how he wanted this to be a much better video than the one for "Heaven."

"Wait, *you* guys wrote 'Heaven'?" I yelled. "Heaven" was one of my favorite pop hits of last summer. Warrant, it turned out, were the toast of the hair scene. Big riffs, pop hooks, party-time metal—the girls loved it. To many, Warrant were the purest embodiment of latter-day L.A. hair metal. With "Cherry Pie," they were about to score the biggest of their three Top 10 singles.

"Quit tickling me," I yelled at Jani as we rolled around on the sheets in front of the camera, smudging my makeup. That Jani was into me was obvious to everyone on set. When I gyrated my hips in my teeny-tiny shorts, shaking my bleached-blond hair around for the camera, I could feel Jani smile.

"Oh, man, Jani *really* likes you," said Kathy Conan, who was married to Warrant's lead guitarist, Joey Allen. All the Warrant girlfriends were on set, and they were sweet as . . . pie. "This video is going to be huge," said Kathy, exchanging numbers with me. Of course I agreed with her, just to be polite. From experience, I figured it would pop up on MTV for a little while and then disappear, like the other videos I had done so far.

In November 1990, "Cherry Pie" hit the radio waves, followed by the world premiere of the video on MTV. I was home in my pajamas with Matthew, watching.

"I'm not sure how many of my scenes they're going to use, probably just one or two," I told Matthew, taking a handful of popcorn.

The video opened with Jani spinning like a wheel, his polka-dot shirt open, black jeans tight.

"Hm," muttered Matthew.

A flash of me, in the red bustier, red lipstick, and denim shorts.

"You look nice, babe," he said. There I was as a roller waitress with a slice of pie, tripping over Joey's guitar cable. Then the pie landed in my lap. There I was in a baseball outfit, there I was in a tight black dress on the couch. Oh, and now they're hosing me down.

"Wow, there's like, more Bobbie Brown than Warrant in this video," said Matthew.

Me and Jani in bed.

"Well, congratulations, Bobbie," said Matthew, trying his best to sound upbeat.

"Cherry Pie" stayed at the top of the video charts for six months, and was in heavy rotation on MTV for almost a year. People thought it was outrageous, and a Canadian cable-TV music network refused to air it because it was "offensively sexist." Which seemed ridiculous to me. The controversy made no sense to me—it was a sexy, playful little video for a sexy, playful song. Of course, the media commentary, good and bad, only benefited both me and the band. "Cherry Pie" was a hit for Warrant, and Bobbie Brown, the Cherry Pie girl, became a star.

I couldn't go anywhere without hearing, "Hey, Cherry Pie!" I still get it to this day. Tawny Kitaen, Whitesnake video babe, had paved the way, but with my more contemporary bubblegum-pop look, I became the poster child for early-'90s hair vixens. To my relief, I noticed that no one, absolutely no one, seemed to care about the *Star Search* debacle. In fact, doors were opening for me in ways I had been dreaming about all my life. The only door closing was on Matthew and me.

Unbeknownst to me, both Gunnar and his record label had been putting pressure on Matthew to break up with me. They feared my influence on him. I was opinionated, and if I didn't like Matthew's stage clothes, I would tell him, and he would listen. If I didn't like a song, I would say so, and Matthew would bring it up with Gunnar. Which made Gunnar very nervous—the whole point of Nelson was that they were hair metal angels who *matched*. The last thing he needed was a Southern-fried Yoko Ono on his hands, messing with the program. Gunnar set about edging me out by making me feel as uncomfortable as possible.

Gunnar was constantly trying to initiate a threesome, for example, with me, him, and his brother. Thankfully, Matthew said no and stood his ground. They had had three-ways together in the past, but when it came to me, Matthew wasn't sharing. Even if he had been interested, I had told Matthew about my creepy almost ménage à trois with Steve and the lesbian, and had already made it clear I was not in the market for group sex. So Gunnar came up with other ways to try my patience. He would call me to come in his bedroom, and I'd walk in to find him naked on the bed. His girlfriend Laurel would casually walk in on me and take off her top. One night, the four of us were watching a movie when Laurel climbed on top of Gunnar and took all her clothes off. Then Gunnar started fingerbanging her, like, no biggie. I nudged Matthew in disbelief.

"Why are we okay with this?" I whispered. "Should we leave? What the fuck!"

I got up, left the room, and got in the shower. The bathroom was the only place I felt safe.

"Hey, you better quit eating all that cherry pie, Bobbie, you're getting fat."

Gunnar had burst in on me and was ogling my body.

"Get the fuck out of here, Gunnar!" I screamed.

Eventually, I knew I'd have to tell Matthew about his twin brother's behavior. I dreaded the conversation. To make things worse, it seemed like we couldn't escape "Cherry Pie."

"And here we go again!" Matthew would half laugh, as the song came on the car radio for the millionth time that day. Deep down I knew he was threatened by Warrant's success, and my connection to it. Then Jani really threw a spanner in the works.

My agent called me, sounding half frantic, half amused. "Um, did you tune into *The Howard Stern Show* today, Bobbie?"

"No. Why?"

"Well, Warrant were on the show, and Jani was talking about you."

"What did he say?"

"He said he didn't care who Matthew Nelson thinks he is, because he is in love with you and is going to marry you. Mr. Cherry Pie wants his Mrs. Cherry Pie, Bobbie."

I couldn't believe Jani—surely this had to be a joke. Right? Reluctantly, I told Matthew, before he found out from someone else.

"Ugh. Why would Jani say something like that?" he asked, looking sad. Gunnar was more direct.

"Why don't you just fuck Jani already and put him out of his misery? Unless you already have, that is!" Some days, I really hated Gunnar. It felt like he didn't want his brother to be happy.

It was true that Jani had been calling me a lot. Sometimes I would come home from work to find him hanging out with my roommate at our apartment. As soon as I walked in the room, all his attention would be focused on me. It was obvious he had a crush, and it was a little awkward—but now, with this radio shit, I had to put a stop to his flirting before people started getting the wrong idea. The next time Jani called me, I told him to lose my number. I reminded him that I already had a boyfriend. "I have your number, and I will use it if I want to, Jani." He was crushed.

BOBBIE, MEET PAMELA

"Hey, Bobbie, check out *Star* magazine; you're in it!" said Tracey Mikolas, head model booker at Flame.

Later that day at the supermarket, I grabbed a copy of *Star* and looked through the pages. What was Tracey talking about? *Ah.* There she was, my doppelgänger. A model by the name of Pamela Anderson, photographed with Scott Baio.

Who is she? And why is she hanging with Baio? I wondered.

Pamela was five foot seven, I was five foot eight, and we were both blond bombshells with surfer girl appeal. She was two years older than me but had arrived in Hollywood the same year I did, 1989, after being spotted in the crowd at a BC Lions game in Vancouver, wearing a tight Labatt's shirt. Hugh Hefner had made her his October 1989 *Playboy* cover girl, so she moved to L.A., got a boob job, and was trying to make it big as a model. In 1990, just after I shot the "Cherry Pie" video, she and I were cast alongside each other. I was excited to meet my lookalike.

I met her on the set of *Married . . . with Children*, where we were playing Al Bundy's fantasy blondes.

"Hey, I'm Bobbie," I said.

"Hey," said Pamela, flashing a quick smile and looking over my shoulder. She seemed disinterested. *About as friendly as a cornered rat,* I thought. *Oh well. Maybe she's just shy.*

In Al Bundy's fantasy, Pamela and I were among four women lavishing him with attention on the couch, Pamela by one knee and me at his other. Pamela would not stop stroking his leg up and down.

Pamela and I were blond girls with dreams, except I was perhaps more naïve than she. There were so many lessons I had yet to learn. How desirability will gain you admirers, but rarely will it gain you true love. How beauty opens many doors, but you should beware of where they lead. Pamela was more switched on to the realities of the game we were playing, as confident and self-assured as I seemed. I didn't realize Hollywood could chew you up and spit you out just as quickly as it could fool you into believing you're the hottest girl in town. I thought I was too special to get hurt, too down-to-earth to get suckered in.

HAWAII

"So *did* you sleep with Jani, Bobbie? Is that how you got the job?" Matthew's eyes flashed. I had never seen him so angry. Things with him and me had hit rock bottom. I couldn't believe that the tender lover who used to stroke my hair until I fell asleep at night was turning on me in this way.

We were four days into a vacation in Hawaii, and despite the rainbows, sunsets, and turquoise waters, things were ugly as can be. Matthew was still bitter about Jani's gallant marriage proposal on *The Howard Stern Show*, even though I had argued that it was just for publicity, to bring attention to the video and the song. And Jani had sparked other, completely unfounded suspicions in Matthew's mind.

"Bobbie, I need to know what happened between you and Richard Grieco. Were you intimate with him, too? Gunnar told me he has photos."

Gunnar had concocted some cock-and-bull story involving me and the actor Richard Grieco, which, like everything else that came out of Gunnar's mouth, was a crock. Yes, I had met Richard at the Roxbury. And yes, he had asked for my number. So had Johnny Depp; so had Paul Stanley from Kiss (he was so effeminate, I assumed he was gay); so had a lot of guys in town. But I had hoped that by now, Matthew would have understood that I didn't play around. It wasn't fair that Gunnar was doing this to me, and to Matthew.

"Matthew, I have to tell you something. I wouldn't believe everything Gunnar tells you. The truth is, he has been coming on to me."

There, I said it.

Matthew was horrified. I knew he didn't believe me. And even if he had, ultimately it wouldn't have mattered. Blood is thicker than water, and in the heat of the moment, I had forgotten that nothing, not even love, was going to get in the way of Matthew and Gunnar Nelson's careers.

"You should go home, Bobbie," said Matthew, his voice cracking. "I can't do this anymore."

He helped me pack some clothes; then he drove me to the airport. "Are you okay?" he asked me. I couldn't even speak. I got on the first plane back to L.A., and cried the entire five-hour flight. Matthew had asked me to have my belongings out of the house by the time they got back from Hawaii, so as to avoid any further confrontation. Which gave me about three days to get my shit out. Tracey, my booker at Flame, came over and helped me pack up.

"Tracey, I'm so fucking hurt," I said, shoving clothes into a duffel bag.

"Don't get mad, Bobbie. Get even."

An interesting proposition. *What would really get under Matt's skin,* I wondered?

In a coat pocket, I found Kathy Conan's number. She was the sweet girlfriend of Warrant's guitarist.

"Hey, Kathy, so Matthew and I broke up. Just wanted to let you know."

Exactly five minutes after Kathy and I hung up, the phone rang.

"Hello?"

"Hey, Bobbie, it's Jani Lane."

Chapter Six

SHE'S MY CHERRY PIE

"This song is for Miss Bobbie Brown!"

Jani Lane dedicated "Heaven," Warrant's huge lighters-in-the-air ballad to me on our first date. As the stage lights exploded in Shreveport, Louisiana, I surveyed the screaming fans and privately noted that Matthew Nelson had never, not once, publicly dedicated a song to me.

"Jani's so intense!" said my friend Tammy, who had come with me to the show. "He looks like he really means it, you know?"

"Uh-huh," I said, imagining Matthew's face when he found out the Cherry Pie guy had dedicated a song to the Cherry Pie girl onstage. For a second, I wondered if maybe Jani was pursuing me as a publicity stunt—but no, Jani didn't seem desperate enough for that. Manufacturing a love affair to boost record sales just didn't seem his style.

Jani had bought me a ticket from Los Angeles to New Orleans. I figured I'd kill two birds with one stone, combine my date with Jani with a visit back home. I hadn't been back since leaving two years ago, and Baton Rouge seemed so dull. My mom and Mr. Earl were just the same. The house was just the same. Everything was the same, except that I couldn't step out the door without people recognizing me from *Star Search* or the "Cherry Pie" video. *Wow, am I famous?* I thought. *Maybe.*

Tammy and I made the swampy four-hour drive north from Baton Rouge to Shreveport, past small church towns and old plantations. By the time we arrived, my skin was sticky and hot. "I forgot about this damn Southern heat," I said, splashing my face at a water fountain in the parking lot.

Warrant had just taken the stage in front of the packed venue. For all the rocker posturing, there was more to Jani Lane than the façade. He was truly charismatic. It was something to do with the way he moved, the way he commanded the stage. When he smiled, the room smiled with him. After the show, Tammy and I met up with Jani and the Warrant guys at a local bar. We drank Coors and shot pool. No velvet ropes, no VIP rooms. When the bar closed, the band called a taxi to take them to their hotel—they had to leave early the next morning to get to their next show.

"I want to come home with you, Bobbie," said Jani.

"What about your show tomorrow?" I said.

"I'll catch a plane, don't worry about it. I want to fall asleep next to you."

Tammy, Jani, and I went back to our motel room in Shreveport. Tammy passed out immediately in one of the two beds, and Jani and I lay together in the other. He was running his hand up and down my side, kissing my neck, tugging softly on my jeans. I unbuttoned them, and he pulled them down, then my panties. All thoughts of Matthew drifted away as Jani unbuckled his pants and slowly, quietly, did what we'd both been thinking about all night.

In the morning, I acted like it was nothing. In the early '90s, sexual mores were still just as freewheeling as they had been in the '80s. You could sleep with someone on the first date and own it. As Jani waited for his taxi to take him to the airport, he said he wanted to see me again.

"Let me fly you out next time I play a show?" he said, taking my hands and kissing me.

"Maybe."

On our way back from Shreveport, I made Tammy pull over at a small occult shop I had visited a few times in the past. Inside was a guy who looked like your average Joe, but he was a voodoo doctor, the real deal. My grandpa John had told me witch doctors would go into the swamps to dig up roots and wild plants for their medicines and potions. He told me about women who made magical dolls, and about the power of New Orleans gris-gris. I had grown up with my head swimming with tales of hoodoo, rootwork, and Southern conjure. I believed in magic, and I still do.

"I want you to cast a spell on Matthew Nelson that takes away his money, love, and success," I told the voodoo doctor. "You have to be careful with revenge spells—sometimes they come back around," he said. "Are you sure?"

"I'm sure." He gave me a black fabric voodoo doll, a black

candle, and some black-arts oil. Then he wrote down some instructions.

When I got back to L.A., I spent nine days in my newly rented apartment performing magic. "First, anoint the black candle with the oil," read the instructions. I had to burn the candle for seventeen minutes each day, for nine days. While it burned, I held the candle in my left hand and cursed Matthew Nelson, dripping the wax all over the doll's body. It stared back at me with its helpless button eyes.

"May Nelson's career suck forever!"

"May Matthew Nelson never love anyone more than me!"

After the ninth day of incantations, I put what was left of the candle in a small box along with the doll, a small bottle of rum, and nine cents. I wrapped it in black cloth and tied it with twine. I was supposed to take it to a cemetery and bury it, but that was too creepy. So I shoved it behind some boxes and asked the black-magic gods to get to work ASAP.

AN ITEM

"So, Bobbie, we hear you've been seeing someone."

I was being interviewed live on KROQ, L.A.'s biggest rock music radio station. Sometimes the DJs would call me and ask me questions about what was happening on the Strip.

Had someone photographed me with Jani in Shreveport maybe? *Oh well, the cat's out of the bag,* I thought.

"Yes, we heard you were at the Cathouse last night, making out with Taime Downe."

What the fuck?

Taime Downe was the lead singer of a hair band called Faster Pussycat and he looked like a Nazi tranny. The Cathouse was his club with Riki Rachtman, host of MTV's *Headbangers Ball*, pure sleaze, full of fast sex and hairspray. It was the dirtiest, most punk rock of the Hollywood clubs. Lita Ford had puked in the bathroom. Christina Applegate worked coat check. Slash fell down the stairs. Axl wore a Cathouse T-shirt in the "Paradise City" video. Every seedy hair metal cliché you can think of had happened at the Cathouse. But never, not once, did I swap spit with Taime Downe.

"Dude, Taime had something in his eye and I was trying to see what it was!" I protested. Fucking journalists. Later that day, the phone rang again. This time it was Jani. "So what's this about you and Taime? Did you guys seriously hook up?" Jani was on the road, somewhere in Oregon. One of his buddies had heard me on the radio and called him. News travels fast. "Um, *no*. I don't kiss drag queens," I said.

Taime wore way too much lipstick for my taste. And he was just an acquaintance. Jani promised he believed me, and we hung up. *Wait, why is Jani acting all boyfriendy?* I thought. We hadn't had an official conversation about our relationship— apart from him asking me to marry him live on national radio, that is.

A few days later, Jani called me again from the road. He had found a phone booth and called me long-distance. "The show was awesome, and our video is number one on MTV," he said, excited. "Oh, and Bobbie, I love you."

"Wait, what?" Then he hung up the phone.

On my twenty-first birthday, October 7, Jani presented me with a platinum and diamond bracelet he had bought in Beverly Hills with the help of my model booker, Tracey. It was the most beautiful piece of jewelry I had ever seen.

"Bobbie, I think you should move in with me," he said.

Whoa.

It felt like things were happening really fast. Jani was always talking about "when we're married" this and "when we're married" that. "Just say the word, Bobbie. I'm your guy." But I had not given marriage any serious thought since T-Boy broke my heart in high school. I felt too young to be locked down.

A few days later, I went out of town on a modeling job. When I got home, my apartment was empty. Couch, tables, bed—gone. There was a note on the carpet.

Your new palace awaits.

There was an address on the back . . . Jani had gone ahead and moved me into his place while I was away! I got in my car and headed over to his house in Sherman Oaks. I was less furious than you might imagine. Actually, I was flattered—having been dumped by Matthew Nelson because he was too weak to stand up against his brother, it was refreshing to meet a guy who so clearly knew what he wanted. Me. I was used to getting

attention from men, but Jani was more devoted, more chival-
rous than any other guy I had met. His fervent belief that I was
"the one" was alluring. I had already been let down by a string
of men, and his adoration made me feel safe. Plus I admired his
chutzpah.

I knocked on the door, and Jani opened it, smiling.

"See? Your stuff looks awesome here," he said.

"I didn't know breaking and entering was a hobby of yours."

"It wasn't, until I met you."

I wished I could have called Matthew there and then. "Hey,
asshole, guess what: I'm with someone who is more famous than
you, who worships me and adores me and isn't afraid to tell the
whole world." Jani had no qualms about standing up onstage
and telling everyone that Bobbie Brown was the most beautiful
girl in the room. Thanks to this kind of gallantry I was becoming
putty in Jani's hands. He knew how to push all the right buttons. It wasn't so much a physical attraction for me, with Jani,
as it was an emotional attraction. Whether or not for the right
reasons, I was definitely falling in love.

I looked around Jani's house. It was a sweet place, a family
home, with a yard. "Well, I guess I'm here now." I sat on the
couch—my couch. Actually, it wasn't so bad in here. He'd deco-
rated it pretty nice. It was bright and warm. "Hey, so I found this
weird thing at your place," said Jani. "I wasn't sure what to do
with it." He pointed at the display cabinet where, alongside his
high school track-and-field trophies, my voodoo doll sat, staring back at me.

Yikes!

As soon as Jani left the room, I grabbed it and tossed it in the trash. I wasn't going to let myself think about Matthew Nelson anymore. That chapter was closed.

LOVE SHACK

Living with Jani was fun. Well, it was fun at first. Fashion had always been my thing, and he loved to be styled. When I met him on the "Cherry Pie" set, he had his jeans tucked into his cowboy boots, complete with moose-knuckle. *Oh, no, no, no,* I thought. Within a few weeks of living together, I was helping him update his look. I got him in some hip-hugger leather pants made that laced at the side and didn't go up to his boobs. He stopped wearing bicycle shorts, tank tops, and groovy white George Michael jackets. We trimmed his hair so it was less straggly (he would come to me for haircuts for the rest of his life), and we threw out the fanny packs and the goofy hats. He looked one thousand times cooler, and he told me he loved his new look. It was fun playing dress-up with Jani.

"What are your fantasies?" Jani asked me one night. We were in bed, snuggling.

"What if we had a ménage à trois?" I suggested. With Jani, I felt safe enough to try it again, if that was what he wanted. At this point, I kind of assumed that was what *all* rock stars wanted.

Jani nearly fell out of the bed. "No way, Bobbie! Really?"

"Well, what's *your* fantasy?" I was defensive now.

"I don't know, you wearing high heels naked, standing in a shopwindow?"

"Oh."

Even though he was a rock star, Jani was kind of a sex newbie, a down-home boy. I already had a fair amount of experimenting under my belt. He had had one threesome before and hated it. Thankfully, he wasn't a talker, nor did he expect me to talk. He was a very quiet lover, and sometimes the only way I could tell he was having an orgasm was by listening to his breathing. Also, I couldn't go anywhere near his ass. That especially freaked him out. He wasn't into foreplay, and never, ever went down on me. (After he and I separated, apparently that was *all* he was about, I heard through the grapevine via his subsequent wives.) When we were in bed, I was either blowing him or fucking him, and with no other stimulation on the table, I started to get frustrated.

While I was getting pissed off about what was happening in our bedroom, Jani was increasingly annoyed by the guys lurking outside it. I don't think I have ever had a boyfriend who hasn't been bummed out by the army of guy friends that I keep within a five-mile radius. I keep my guy buddies close, probably too close for comfort. But I wasn't a cheater, and I assumed that Jani knew that too. So I couldn't understand why he would get so upset about all my platonic boyfriends, like Slash from Guns N' Roses.

I had met Slash at a party and went up to him and moved

his hair away from his face, like it was a curtain. He was kind of shy and seemed to be using his hair as a mask.

"Wow, you're actually really cute, Slash!"

Slash and I started talking on the phone during the day, like grandmas. We would watch cooking shows together, and soaps. He was useless at sewing, so I would sew the buttons on his jeans. Harmless shit. But Jani hated it. "If you like Slash so much, why don't you have his babies," he grouched, and I just rolled my eyes. I had yet to have a boyfriend who didn't act like he wanted to own me.

Jani was equally pissed about my friendship with Jay Gordon. Jay was this punky glam kid from San Francisco who played bass guitar and, like everyone else in town, dreamed about being a rock star. He was my age but seemed younger, and was tapped into a new, alternative metal sound. He was good friends with a guy called Jonathan Davis, who would become famous for his band Korn and would sign Jay and his band Orgy to his record label, turning Jay into an industrial-metal pinup. But that was a whole decade away, and when I met Jay, he was just a gangly cute kid who liked to dance.

"Where's Jani?" Jay asked me, one of the first times we met, on the dance floor at Spice. "Oh, Jani *hates* dancing," I said, shrugging. "I'll dance with you!" said Jay. We tore it up. Anyone who could keep up with me on the dance floor was a friend for life, in my opinion, and Jay, like me, was a club kid in the truest sense. He loved heavy metal but he dug electronica too; he knew his hip-hop, and he looked exotic. I had a feeling we would be in each other's lives for a long time. Jani glanced over at Jay. He seemed uncomfortable. "Can't you just find some girl-friends to dance with, Bobbie? Please?"

I was partying more and more, pissing off my long-suffering manager and agent. Every time I failed to show for a meeting, I would avoid their irate calls and just send them a fax with "I'M SORRY" written in big letters. My manager, Janis Hansen, a former *Playboy* Bunny who founded a successful talent agency, almost dumped me several times. Especially after my audition with Steven Spielberg.

I had been invited to read for the part of Tinkerbell in Steven Spielberg's action adventure *Hook*. The casting agent informed us that the role had gone to Julia Roberts but that Spielberg still wanted to meet with me, because he was interested in casting me as one of the mermaids. But I kept rescheduling my meeting with Mr. Spielberg, like a dumbass.

"Bobbie, you know it was kind of rude of you to keep rescheduling on us," said Steven, when I finally managed to make time to meet him. "People don't do that to me very often. But I'd still like you to read for this part; I think you could be great in it."

"Yeah, well, I'm here now!" I said. "Let's read this thing!"

The double shots of whiskey I had downed to calm my nerves were having the opposite effect I had hoped for, and I was drunk as a skunk. I started twirling around and around on the office chair.

"Bobbie . . . are you okay?" said Steven. No, I was not okay,

I was behaving like a fruitcake, being an obnoxious dick to one of the most respected film directors in the world. Mr. Spielberg did not call me back. Go figure.

"Every time you get in a relationship, all of a sudden you don't give a fuck about your career and your guy is the only thing you care about. Have you noticed that, Bobbie?" My manager was *pissed*. It was true, but I shrugged it off, like I did all my failures and fuckups. My life was supposed to be effortless and carefree, full of glamorous rock star boyfriends and fun times—that was my image, after all. Every time I let myself care about career opportunities, I had to face my deep-rooted fear that, underneath it all, maybe I wasn't good enough, pretty enough, smart enough, or lovable enough for any of this. It was much safer for me to laugh and pretend I didn't care and act like having ambition was dumb and uncool, while burying myself in my relationship. In Hollywood, that kind of immature bravura will only get you so far. The models and actresses around me who knew what they wanted and took their goals seriously would slowly but surely overtake me as I sabotaged every major opportunity that came my way. Every time.

I had been talking to Jive Records about possibly signing with the label and launching a pop career. They had seen me on *Star Search* and were looking for a cute Southern girl to groom into a pop princess. I had met with them several times, done voice tests at their studios, and met with their choreographers. My voice was okay, not amazing, but they especially loved the way I danced. Jani was confused.

"You're not even a singer—how come *you're* getting a record deal?"

The whole thing ruffled his feathers, because it underscored everything he hated about the music business. He and so many of the other musicians he knew had worked incredibly hard to get their record deals. So how come someone like me, a pretty face who never even wanted to be a singer, could have serious offers on the table? I wasn't surprised at all, though. Things had always landed in my lap—from winning my first pageant to landing a modeling contract to becoming the Cherry Pie girl who got the Cherry Pie boy to being courted by Jive Records: I had never had to work for any of it. And I would only miss those opportunities once they were gone.

ローション

When Warrant toured Japan in the spring of 1991, I went with the band as Jani's companion for the entire monthlong tour. He wanted me with him as much as possible, probably because he was worried about the boys I was hanging out with when he wasn't around. I unpacked my bag in the hotel room and realized I had forgotten my birth control pills. *Fuck.* I walked to the nearest pharmacy and tried to explain what I needed. Spermicide would cover it, I figured. Unfortunately the word for "spermicide" was not in my Japanese phrase book. I stood in front of the little old Japanese lady pharmacist using some improvised sign language for "sex" and "birth control." After a while, she seemed to get it and nodded enthusiastically. She handed me a tube of gel with some writing on the side of it that I could not understand.

ローション

What the fuck is "ローション"? I said. She shrugged.

Well, at least it had the same number of letters as "sperm." I paid and waved good-bye to the old Japanese lady.

A few days later, Jani and I were on the bullet train, speeding at two hundred miles per hour across the Japanese countryside. I had brought the spermicide in my bag. We snuck into the tiny bathroom and he pulled up my dress and unbuckled his jeans. We had sex up against the bathroom door, traveling at close to the speed of sound. "This is crazy," I giggled as he kissed me over and over.

I stayed with the band through the rest of the Japanese tour, through Australia, and then across the Pacific back to Los Angeles. A few weeks after we got home, Jani and I were at the grocery store and he leaned across my chest to grab some tomatoes. I squealed.

"Ouch, my boob! It really hurts! What if I have boob cancer?"

"Bobbie, you don't have boob cancer."

I hadn't gone back on my pills yet, and we were still using the spermicide I had bought in Tokyo. Even so, something didn't feel quite right. I was bummed out. I was sleeping constantly. I felt gaggy around seafood. Keiko, a Japanese-American model friend of mine, came over one day. I showed her the tube of

Japanese spermicide. Maybe that was what was making me feel sick? Maybe they made it with whale blubber?

"Bobbie, 'ローション' is Japanese for 'lotion,'" said Keiko, looking at the tube. "You know, lube?"

I took a pregnancy test and BOOM. Positive. I couldn't believe it—the doctors in Baton Rouge had told me I would probably never be able to have children after the surgery to get rid of the cancer in my cervix just a few years earlier. I called my mom immediately. "I know Jani and I have only been together a few months but . . . we're having a baby!"

My mom, ever intuitive, could sense the giddiness in my voice. Things had moved faster with Jani than anyone had expected. She said something that surprised me. "You know, Bobbie, you don't have to get married if you don't want to. You can have the baby, and there are plenty of people in your life who love you and will help you." I mulled over her words. "No, Mom, my baby needs a father."

"I support you in whatever decision you make," she said.

Not for a second did I consider not going through with the pregnancy. And Jani was thrilled, even though we had only been together four months. "Now you *have* to marry me, right?" he said, kissing me. He formally proposed over dinner at our favorite Italian restaurant, Miceli's in Hollywood, surrounded by singing Italian waiters. In our dessert was a ring. Without hesitation, I said yes. We planned to marry that coming July.

As soon as Jive, the record label, found out that I was

knocked up and about to get hitched, they withdrew their offer of a deal. (It took them a few years, but eventually they found the unpregnant Southern pop princess they had been looking for—her name was Britney Spears.) My modeling agency was equally irritated that I was pregnant so early in my career. They warned me that being married with a child is a real setback for a young model. I thought about all the hair metal videos and catalog shoots I would be missing out on and laughed. As far as I was concerned, this baby was a gift straight from heaven.

Once word spread that I was pregnant and marrying Jani, Matthew finally decide to get in touch.

"Bobbie?" A lump formed in my throat as I recognized the voice on the end of the line. Matthew sounded depressed. He had been talking to my mom in the aftermath of our breakup, and confessed to her how Gunnar and his management had been pressuring him to break up with me all along. Now he regretted not standing up to them. Matthew told me that he still loved me and that he had made a mistake. "Please don't marry Jani. Go with love, don't take this other path. It's a mistake."

"Matthew, I'm pregnant. Things are different now."

"Perhaps there are ways we can get around that."

"You're crazy! You had your chance, Matthew. I'm not aborting my baby, if that's what you mean. No way."

In that moment I had, unequivocally, steered my life's path away from anything involving Matthew Nelson. The future, I knew, lay with Jani Lane.

WEDDING BELLS

Jani and I were married on July 27, 1991, in a fairy-tale Hollywood wedding, an explosion of silk, balloons, tulle, and champagne on the rooftop of the Wyndham Bel Age hotel. As the
afternoon faded into evening over the Sunset Strip, the air filled
with the soft, intoxicating fragrance of hundreds of pale pink
Sterling Silver roses, among the sweetest-smelling flowers in the
world. We had a decadent three-tier wedding cake, and I wore
a wedding gown I designed with famous Beverly Hills bridal
stylist Renée Strauss, who also styled the weddings of Dennis
Hopper, Raquel Welch, Gary Oldman, and even the famous
wedding scene starring Stephanie Seymour in the video for the
Guns N' Roses song "November Rain."

As my father walked me down the aisle, I realized that this
day wasn't about the cake or the dress or the gorgeous flowers or the centerpiece or my bridal veil. I felt our baby move
in my belly, and something in me shifted—Bobbie Brown the
freewheeling woman-child was faced with something she hadn't
experienced before. Adulthood. I smiled broadly at Jani as the
ordained minister pronounced us man and wife. As we kissed in
front of our guests, my heart pounded. I was only twenty-three,
but this was some real, grown-up shit that was happening.

As the evening progressed, the night got wilder and more
surreal. Duff McKagan wandered in late after a Guns N' Roses
gig and then got up onstage with Jani to sing a version of "Hey
Joe." Rick Allen, Def Leppard's drummer, was there, as were
all the guys from Warrant, of course. Bobby Brown, the R & B

singer, and my club buddy, came up to congratulate me. "So, where *did* you get the name Bobbie Brown?" he asked me, and I pointed at my father. "I was named after my dad." He thought that was the coolest thing ever. "If I ever have a daughter, I am going to name her after me," he said, and true to his word, on March 4, 1993, when Whitney Houston gave birth to their only child, he named her Bobbi Kristina Brown.

My father, unlike the rest of the wedding party, had driven all the way from Baton Rouge to the wedding. His whole life, he hated to fly. It wasn't anything to do with not wanting to sit with my mom and Mr. Earl on an airplane. It had taken a few years, but thanks to Mr. Earl's gracious and open nature, they had all become friends. My father would even go to Sunday dinner with my mom and Mr. Earl at their house. Mr. Earl had done so much to raise us and help our family, my mom had wondered if he should walk me down the aisle as well as my father. "You know, like walk you halfway down," she suggested. My mom was always practical like that. I thought about it and decided against the idea. "No matter what happened in the past, I don't want to hurt Dad's feelings, not on a day like this," I said. "I support you in whatever you decide" was her response.

Because I was already three months pregnant, I was too tired to party with everyone else until late, so I went home and climbed in to bed, exhausted. I lay there, waiting for Jani, my husband. My mind was spinning. "Forever" had been a word I had tossed around before, but now I wondered what that even meant. I thought about my mother and father, about my mother and Mr. Earl. They seemed like grown-ups, the kind of people who knew what "marriage" and "motherhood" were actually supposed to be about. When Jani came home after entertaining our guests all night, we didn't have sex. Instead, we clung to each other in our sleep, dreaming of this new future and what it held for us both.

MY GIRL SHARISE

I was at our house in Sherman Oaks, pregnant, married, and chugging pickle juice. I became *obsessed* with pickle juice throughout my pregnancy—*no wonder Grandpa John called me Pickle*, I thought. Pickle juice, peach juice, caviar on toast, and guacamole. Guacamole every day. And the house was a mess. I was the opposite of a domestic goddess, the Antichrist of home economics—everything I tried to cook tasted like hell, and cleaning was something other people did. I had always been used to just being me, trying to have a career and living in the fast lane. It was hard adjusting to this new pace of life.

As I watched TV and munched on pickles, I paused on some channel that was airing Mötley's "Girls, Girls, Girls" video. Somehow, even though the song had come out four years prior, in 1987, I hadn't seen it. I was transfixed. *Dayum, those girls are hot*, I thought, dipping my pickle in a tub of guac. The video had been banned by MTV because of nudity, which I thought was almost as dumb as that Canadian channel banning "Cherry Pie." Shot at the Seventh Veil strip club in L.A., it features a bunch of strippers with incredibly firm tits and asses bouncing around onstage while Mötley Crüe sit around looking self-satisfied. Tommy looked super cute, as always. But honestly, the girls were cuter.

A couple of nights later, I heard that Vince Neil from Mötley was doing a solo performance at Spice, so I figured I'd haul my tired, pregnant ass over there and drink Shirley Temples, with pickles on the side. Jani was on the road, and I was just dying to get out of the house. I put on a flattering dress and was grateful that at nearly four months, I was still hardly showing. I had been at the club not twenty minutes when Vince approached me.

"I've been wanting to get to know you better, Bobbie," he said, leaning in a little too close. His breath was overpowering. Was this asshole really hitting on me? "Yes, Jani and I were hoping you could have come to our wedding, with your *wife*," I said. By now, his hands were on my ass. "So, where is your *wife*, exactly?" Vince looked nonplussed. "I dunno, Sharise is here somewhere," he grunted, pissed off. I scanned the room and recognized Sharise Neil from the "Girls, Girls, Girls" video. She was a former mud wrestler who had a daughter with Vince, and from what I had heard, she was one sassy broad. "Ah, there she is!"

I wanted to punish Vince for being such a sleazeball, so I marched over to Sharise and introduced myself, with Vince trailing me, in a panic. Sharise was just as gorgeous in the flesh as she had been in the video. "Hey, Sharise, I'm Bobbie," I said, watching Vince squirm. "Vince had such nice things to say about you."

"Oh, really? Well Vince is a cheating son of a bitch," said Sharise. "I give this marriage three months. You hear me, Vince? Now fuck off and let me talk to Bobbie." I was impressed.

BABY BLUES

I don't care what anyone says about being pregnant—unless you're a meadow-skipping earth mama in bare feet, it pretty much sucks. "You're getting kinda fat, Bobbie," Jani pointed out. Jani was not the most tactful husband during my pregnancy, to say the least. Possibly, deep down, he was just as freaked out about what was happening as I was. On top of that, he had always been squeamish, and my swollen belly, my cankles, my constant need to pee, the veins in my tits—the physical changes associated with pregnancy—were grossing him out. It didn't help that I was hornier than ever—and the more I begged him for sex, the more turned off he became. The heady romance that had brought us together in the first place was becoming lost in a sea of maternity wear and pickle juice. My being pregnant, needy, and "fat" was a burden he was not mature enough to deal with.

I retaliated the way I knew best—with words. I have a mean mouth. I can cut a person to the core with my words, and it has been a problem throughout my relationships. But I was pregnant, horny, and mad. If Jani thought I was too fat to be fucked, I was going to make him pay.

"You're such a loser, Jani. You can't even have sex with your wife. I'm sick of sucking dick all the time."

"Is that baby even mine, Bobbie? Or is it gonna come out black like Slash?" He could give as good as he got.

"I guess we'll have to wait and see, huh, Jani?"

One night, when Jani was out on the road, Slash called and invited me to see Guns N' Roses play in downtown Los Angeles. He had no idea that he had been the subject of our arguments. Slash was just a nice guy who felt sorry for me. I was six months along by now and wasn't feeling too sexy, thanks to feeling constantly rejected by Jani. I fought the feelings of panic that welled up inside me from time to time, the sense that maybe I had made a mistake, that I was too young for all this, that I wasn't ready to be a wife, let alone a mother. *Fuck it, I'll go to the show,* I thought. I wanted to feel like a kid again, just for a second.

I showed up at the venue and headed straight to the backstage area to say hi to my buds Slash and Duff. "I know somebody who wants to meet you," Slash said, from behind his curtain of curls. "Really? You've gotta be kidding. I look like Mount fucking Everest." I had forgotten what it felt like to be desired. A familiar thrill flooded my veins. "So . . . who is it?" I asked Slash.

Skid Row was opening for Guns N' Roses that night and their front man, Sebastian Bach, was one of the most beautiful men in rock. A cross between a heavy metal Viking and Lord Byron, he had a romantic, feminine face that was prettier than any girl's. Mine included. I heard a high-pitched scream: "Heyyyy!" It was Sebastian, kicking open the door to the dressing room, in all his pouty, tight-trousered glory. "He's crazy," I whispered to Slash. "Yup." Sebastian's eyes scanned the room, resting on me.

Oh, shit.

He walked toward me, grabbing a handful of ice cubes from a champagne bucket on his way over, then stuffing the ice down my shirt. I almost gave birth on the spot. "Hi, I'm Sebastian," he said. "Will you watch my band tonight?" He had a giant coke booger hanging out of his nose.

I stood side-stage, watching Skid Row play, mesmerized. At one point Sebastian walked over and spat at me, which I believe was his way of saying hi. At the after-party, he was all over me like a rash. Frankly, after months of rejection from Jani, the attention felt good. Suddenly, Sebastian pushed me up against the wall of the dressing room, his hard crotch pushing against the unborn child in my belly. I glanced around the room, but everyone was too wasted to notice. When he stuck his tongue down my throat, I thought I might gag. But I didn't push him away. A few minutes later, he came up for air. "I want to see you again," he slurred. "Sebastian, this isn't a good time," I said, pointing at my belly.

The next night, Guns N' Roses played again, and against my better judgment, I went back. I spotted Sebastian and went over to say hello. "Oh, hey, Bobbie," he said, looking busy. "Meet Maria, my wife." I held out my hand, smiling sweetly, feeling like an idiot. I thought about Jani on the road. I imagined the number of unpregnant, uncomplicated groupies he was probably surrounded by at that very moment. My heart felt heavy with a mix of guilt, jealousy, and resentment. "Nice to meet you, Maria. You really missed a great show last night."

When Jani came home a few days later, I searched for some sign that he still loved me, that he still thought I was beautiful. Kissing Sebastian Bach had reminded me what it felt like to be desired. I just wanted the same from my husband. But Jani seemed more shut down than ever and had thrown himself into his work. He was recording the new Warrant album that he hoped could weather the giant shit storm that was about to hit called grunge. Like the asteroid that crashed into the Earth 66 million years ago, grunge was about to crash-land on the Sunset Strip and wipe out the hair metal dinosaurs overnight.

Jani was an incredibly dedicated musician, though, so it shouldn't have mattered. He was always writing, always recording. He wrote all of Warrant's songs, words, and music. He would even write the parts out for every person in the band and hand them their part to learn. But because he was a cool guy, he still split the publishing with them. "Why are you splitting the publishing? That's your bread and butter," I asked him once. "I understand you want to be their friend, but to give them your publishing when you write all the songs seems crazy." But he would just shrug and say that was the way it was. I felt like the rest of the band took Jani for granted. They would sit back and wait until he had finished writing all the songs and then just show up to record.

Jani's ballads were amazing, and I always thought he really had a real gift as a pop artist. But he was supposed to be glam, because that was what the industry was pushing, even though glam metal was already way past its peak by the time Warrant hit the scene. Jani was self-conscious of being known as the Cherry Pie guy, when, in reality, he had so much more to offer as an artist. Sometimes I felt like he blamed me.

We went to a party one night, and Jani was drinking, as usual, so much so that he was too drunk to drive home. So I drove. Instead of sitting in the passenger seat next to me, he sat in the back and started hurling insults at me. "Why are you treating me like this?" I asked him, hurt by his comments. "Because I can, and I enjoy it." I couldn't believe it. When he drank, something very dark in him came to life.

"You want me to fuck you?" said Jani a few days later when I tried to kiss him. "Is that even possible?" I was eight months in and craving attention. Jani had come home drunk and was not in the mood to be nice to me. These days, he rarely was. Eventually Jani decided to give me what I wanted—but not in the romantic manner I hoped.

"Take your clothes off and kneel on the bed," Jani said. He grabbed some scarves and tied my hands to the frame of our four-poster bed.

"Wow, we are getting kinky tonight," I said.

"Don't move."

Then he took a scarf and gagged me.

"For once in your life, Bobbie, you're gonna shut the fuck up."

Then he started fucking me in the ass. I had never had anal sex before, and wanted him to be gentler with me. Instead, it felt like he was trying to teach me a lesson.

It was like that scene out of *Last Tango in Paris*—cold, impersonal, and animalistic. It didn't feel like Jani. Afterward, he untied me and collapsed next to me, panting. I got up and went to the bathroom and tried to make sense of what had just happened. *I must be such a bitch to have pushed Jani to that point,* I thought. *Maybe this is what I deserve. I better watch my fucking mouth from now on.* I splashed my face and then walked back into the bedroom. Jani was asleep. We never mentioned anything about it ever again. A few days later, when I joked about the incident with a couple of girlfriends, their reactions surprised me.

"What the fuck? That is weird, Bobbie," one said.

"Really?" It hadn't dawned on me that I should be concerned.

"Dude, that is not cool," said the other, shaking her head.

The doubts in my head grew as fast as my belly. I thought back to my life a year ago, realizing I could never have imagined myself a wife and mom-to-be at the age of twenty-two, with a husband whose moods I could no longer understand or predict. Some days, I wondered if I was making the biggest mistake of my life. But there was no turning back now.

WAKE-UP CALL

A few weeks before my due date, we were somewhere in the Midwest, traveling along a lonely freeway in the dead of night, headed toward the next stop on the Warrant tour. Jani and I were asleep in a bunk, with me on the outside so I could easily climb down out of the bed and get to the bathroom. When I was pregnant, my actual life felt like stopgaps in between pee breaks.

We were both sound asleep when the bus swerved violently as the driver tried to avoid something on the freeway. As the bus lurched to one side, it flung me out of the bunk and I landed on the floor. Jani was horrified.

"Bobbie, are you okay?"

"Yes, I think so," I said, half-asleep and confused as to what was happening. But when we got the hotel, I went to the bathroom and realized I was not okay. There was blood on my panties.

"Jani, call an ambulance," I screamed.

Lying on a table in the emergency room, I felt like the star of a bad horror movie. Doctors took my pulse and monitored my heart rate, and tried to stem the increasing flow of blood from my womb. I could see in their eyes that all was not well. Because I'd had the surgery on my cervix a few years prior, it was barely holding the contents of my womb in place. The shock of falling out of the bunk on to the floor had weakened it even further, and I was in danger of going into labor.

"She's losing the baby!" said the surgeon, and my heart froze. In that moment, all my doubts and misgivings about becoming a mother disappeared. It dawned on me that all I wanted, all I needed, was to have my baby. I was crying, screaming, staring wildly at Jani as he held my hand, looking terrified.

"The placenta is tearing away from the uterus," said one of the doctors. "I think we're losing her."

I was sobbing through my oxygen mask. All I could think was to pray out loud and ask for help. "God, please don't make me lose this baby! I promise I will not regret this pregnancy! Please, God!" Then the strangest thing happened. The bleeding just stopped. My heart rate stabilized. The doctor's face relaxed. "I think you're going to be okay," he said. "Both of us?" I asked? "Both of you." From that moment on, I was nothing but grateful for the baby that Jani and I were about to have. Never again would I entertain a single thought of regret.

HAPPY BIRTH DAY

On January 15, the day before my scheduled delivery by Caesarean section, Jani came home with an announcement. "Hey, I decided we are not naming the baby Taylar." We had decided on Taylar five months into the pregnancy, after tossing around alternatives including Tresor (my mom's idea) and Trooper (because of the near miscarriage). "What do you mean, we're not calling her Taylar," I growled. I was watching a movie in bed with my mom, who had flown in to help me with the birth. "I just don't like that name anymore," shrugged Jani, unapologetically.

I could have strangled him. I was huge, I was miserable,

and I was in no mood to renegotiate baby names. I picked up an alarm clock and threw it at Jani's head. He ducked. Then I picked up a pillow and hurled it at him, then a notepad and whatever else I could reach from the bed. *"Our daughter's name is Taylar!"* I yelled. Jani retreated into the kitchen, and my mom followed him. "Well, I guess you guys are keeping that name," she said, giving him a hug, and he nodded.

The following day, my mom, Jani, and I drove to Cedars-Sinai Medical Center in Beverly Hills and prepared to deliver our baby. "I have to do a bikini shoot in two weeks, so make sure the scars are low, and be sure to laser some of the muscle tissue; I want to be skinny after the baby is born," I told the doctor, who rolled her eyes. "Oh, and I don't want to shit in front of anyone." I had heard that 90 percent of the time, when you're having a baby, you crap yourself. *No way am I doing that,* I thought. *No way.*

The doctors had decided to book me for a Caesarean because of my unusually narrow hips. Most women experience pelvic widening during their pregnancy, but mine refused to grow into the birthing kind—I was what they call "all belly." From behind you couldn't even tell that I was pregnant, but if you swiveled me to the side, I had the girth of a Hummer. Toward the end of my pregnancy, it was as though Taylar had taken up my entire body. She would move and it was like an alien was visibly squirming around my stomach. You could see her little hands and feet with her ten toes moving under my skin. It was weird, every time Jani and I fought, Taylar would intervene, by getting the hiccups in my stomach. Jani and I would notice my stomach jumping every two seconds, and nearly always, this would diffuse the tension. To this day, Taylar is incredibly sensitive to emotions.

The doctors set me up facing the door, so that anytime anyone would walk in, it was like a meet 'n' greet with my pussy. "Hey, you guys wanna maybe turn me around?" I pleaded, horrified. But to no avail. Suddenly, I felt nothing beneath my hips—they had given me the epidural. This shit was on. A six-foot-tall black male nurse was assisting. He had to work the baby out of my womb by applying pressure to my belly. He was so big that he broke two of my lower ribs, although at the time, of course, I couldn't feel a thing. Then, at 8:30 A.M. on January 17, 1992, our daughter, Taylar, was born, with a full head of spiky white-blond hair, just like Billy Idol. Seriously, it looked like she had a puppy on her head. "She's got angel hair," gushed the doctor. "No wonder you had so much heartburn, Bobbie—that's always a sign that the baby's going to have hair."

Then the doctor called out, "Does anyone want to see her uterus? It's outside of her body." My mom, of course, said yes. "Oh, it looks like a roast beef," she said.

It took me several weeks of rehab in the hospital before I was able to leave. Jani had gone to Florida to record, so I went back to Baton Rouge with my mom and was there for a couple of months before I saw Jani again. *I'll show you, motherfucker,* I thought, remembering Jani's taunts about my figure. I got ripped. I ate five grams or less of fat per day, and I did cardio five days a week. When Jani showed up in Baton Rouge, he couldn't believe it. My body was in better shape than it ever had been. "Will you put a bikini on and go ask for sugar next door?" he said, floored by my abs. "Sure, asshole."

My mom tried to teach me what she could about being a good mother, and I absorbed it as best I could. I couldn't believe the overwhelming feelings of unconditional love I had for our little baby, Taylar. Upon returning to L.A., I tried to be the best new mom I could be—even though oftentimes it was a solo gig, because Jani was working nonstop, either on the road or in the studio. One day, like a good Valley mom, I decided to take Taylar to the mall. She was less than two months old, and I was excited to show her off in some of the cute outfits I had bought her. I washed all her little rompers and onesies—I had finally figured out how to do laundry properly, and had started a lifelong love affair with fabric conditioner—and picked out the outfit I wanted her to wear. I took it out of the dryer, and it was still just a little damp, which I didn't think was a big deal. I got her dressed and got the stroller together, and we went to the mall. When we came home she was sniffing and crying. As the day progressed, so did her fever. I was horrified and called my mom. "I think I made Taylar sick," I cried, realizing that putting my baby in a slightly damp outfit and wheeling her around an air-conditioned mall probably hadn't been my most genius idea ever. Taylar couldn't sleep well for weeks because her nose was so stuffy, and I had to carry her around on my chest almost twenty-four hours a day until she finally got better.

Each night I would sit and rock her and sing soft lullabies until she fell asleep. By the time she was two, when she still was wasn't able to wind down and go to sleep without having Momma rock her and sing to her for an hour every night, it became a challenge. *I wish you could just fall asleep,* I thought, sitting by her crib, feeling guilty the second I had the thought. I wished Jani could have been more help, but he really wasn't around much in the first few years of Taylar's life. As much as he loved her, it seemed like his head was often elsewhere. Even worse, he was starting to come home drunk almost every night.

I had always thought the drinking was part of the hair metal stage act. The Warrant boys often liked to drink before performances, and it just seemed like a thing that rock stars did. I didn't start suspecting that he had a problem with alcohol until I stopped partying. Then I was able to observe his behavior more clearly. Jani would never drink at home, but he would go out and get belligerently drunk and come home with black eyes from getting in fights. And when he was drunk, he would get dark and angry. He wasn't a fun, celebratory drunk. He would wake me up, accuse me of cheating, wake Taylar up and start her crying. "Fuck this shit, Jani, every time you drink, you're a dick," I told him, exasperated. "If you really think I'm cheating and not home all day changing diapers, then divorce me!"

I didn't get his relationship with alcohol, because I had never liked to be out of control. I never wanted to be that girl in the club bathroom unconscious in her own puke, getting fucked by two dudes. So I didn't really drink to excess. And I didn't realize that when people flip their personalities while they're drinking, like Jani did, it's often a sign of some hidden damage. There's usually something they are trying to emotionally escape from, something that is hurting them. When I was married to Jani, I didn't know about any secret pain he might have been suffering. He never shared his troubles with me. Naïve as this sounds, I had no idea I was living with an alcoholic.

One day, when Taylar was around a year old, Jani was feeding her while I was in the yard. I heard a slap and then the sound of Taylar screaming louder than I had ever heard her scream. I ran into the kitchen.

"What the fuck is she crying for?"

"She won't eat. So I popped her on the hand."

"Are you fucking kidding me, Jani? How would you like it if I force-fed you and then hit you just because you were full? If you *ever* hit her again, I will kill you and bury you in a trailer park! You hear me?"

I was so psycho, it was scaring Jani, I could tell. But I never believed in physical discipline in any way, shape, or form. You don't ever have to hit a child in anger in order to get your point across, or control them. All that does is make the child hate you. I knew that from experience. Jani and I got into a huge row about it, and he smashed his guitar over the coffee table.

"I wear the pants in this family!" he yelled.

"Fuck you, I will crack you over the head with a frying pan and not think twice about it!" I screamed back.

"Great, so I'm not the man, even in my own family!" he screamed, and left, headed for the bar.

Chapter Seven

HAPPILY NEVER AFTER

Jani and I had been married about two years. Although neither one of us wanted to admit it, our marriage was already on very thin ice. I still had a lot of resentment built up from the way he had treated me when I was pregnant, and now I was at the point where I had become disinterested in sex. I would hang out in Taylar's room until after Jani had fallen asleep, develop mystery headaches—anything to avoid being intimate with my husband. I tried talking to my married friends about it. "Do you still have sex with your dude?" I'd ask, and most of them would nod. But I just wasn't attracted to Jani anymore. We had no communication, and our life felt like a fairy tale in which we were mere actors, a prince and princess playing house and keeping secrets. I had started using coke again, here and there at parties, to take my mind off things. It was easier to pretend that nothing was wrong, rather than to acknowledge we had problems.

"You look nice," I said. Jani was checking his hair in the hallway mirror before he left the house. He had a meeting with his attorney and was dressed up real fancy.

"Thanks, baby," said Jani, kissing me on the cheek. "I'll be home soon." The front door closed, and I heard his Mercedes pull out of the driveway. Taylar and I sat in front of the TV and watched *Barney & Friends* on VHS.

About an hour later, the phone rang. It was my friend Stacy. "Bobbie, I hate to be the one to tell you this, but the manager of Tony's Italian restaurant called me and Jani was just there with someone."

"Yeah, he's having lunch with his attorney."

"Well, is his attorney a woman? Because they're making out in the parking lot."

Tony's is a joint on Ventura Boulevard. I hadn't been there in a while, but the manager and I had known each other since my early days in L.A. "Who is she?" I said quietly. I couldn't believe this was happening.

"Some asshole named Shannon, apparently."

Shannon, Shannon . . . oh, *Shannon*. She was dating Robbie Crane, who used to be in Ratt and was now in Vince Neil's new solo band. Jani and Shannon had seemed to get along okay— they shot pool together one night, I remembered. She was a model, a brunette with light eyes and a slim figure. I hadn't felt threatened by her at all, so confident was I of Jani's devotion, but I had noticed that she seemed to compliment Jani a lot. And Jani had always been a sucker for a quick ego-boost.

A few hours later, Jani strolled in the door and laid his keys down. I had put Taylar to bed early. "I'm home! Man, it's hot out there. I need a shower." Jani went into our bedroom and started

My father, Bobby Gene Brown,
as a rough and tumble youth.

High school yearbook photo of my
mother, Judy Ann Faul, age sixteen.

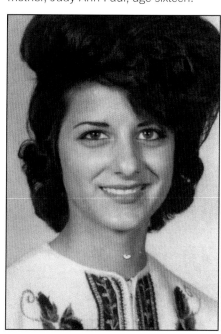

Me, around age three.

Me, around age nine, holding my baby
brother, Adam, almost one. He is still the
apple of my eye, and the sweetest man
I know.

My
brother,
Adam,
and I.
I had just
turned
twenty.

Me, at the Miss Teen
USA pageant.

My first modeling card at Flame, the L.A. agency
that launched my music video career.

My mom, Judy Ann Faul, and
Mr. Earl, while they were dating,
on a trip to Vegas.

My father, Bobbie Gene Brown, walked me down the aisle the day I married Jani Lane. It was a beautiful day for us all.

Me, big as a house.

Me, pregnant with Taylar. Jani had drawn something silly on my belly.

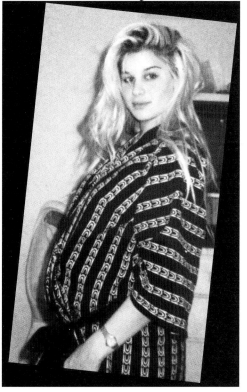

Taylar loved it when my mom put her hair in curlers, even when she was a baby. Funnily enough, I had always hated it.

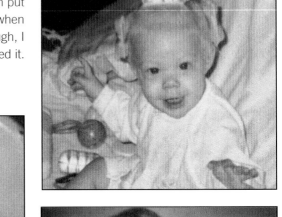

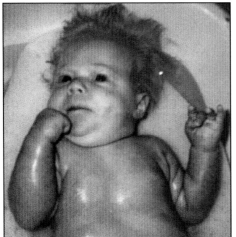

Our daughter, Taylar, was born with an amazingly full head of blond hair. We used to joke she looked like Billy Idol.

Jani and baby Taylar.

Tommy and I loved to **kiss** with our mouths open, because when we were together, we were always laughing.

Tommy and I on vacation in Cancun. Less than a year later, he would marry my rival Pamela Anderson right there on the beach.

Tommy and I in bed in Cancun, shortly after the thing we did best . . . **sex.**

Tommy and I loved to smoke after getting down and dirty.

Tommy loved playing with my daughter Taylar. . . . He always was a big kid.

Tommy,
Taylar,
and I,
on tour.

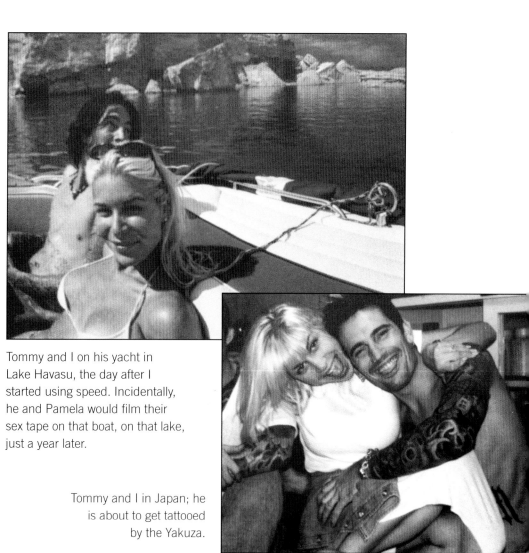

Tommy and I on his yacht in Lake Havasu, the day after I started using speed. Incidentally, he and Pamela would film their sex tape on that boat, on that lake, just a year later.

Tommy and I in Japan; he is about to get tattooed by the Yakuza.

Taylar looked so much like her daddy as a child, and she still does.

Jani with his two daughters:
Taylar on the left and Madison
on the right.

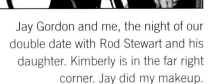

Jay Gordon and me, the night of our
double date with Rod Stewart and his
daughter. Kimberly is in the far right
corner. Jay did my makeup.

Some
friendships
never die.

Sharise and I in 2013.

getting undressed. I followed him and sat on the edge of the bed. "So how was your meeting?"

"It was great. We came up with some good ideas."

"So I have a friend that runs this restaurant and he said that you were there with Shannon. Is that true, Jani?" Jani carried on unbuttoning his shirt. "Don't be crazy, Bobbie." His voice was higher than usual. "Well, Tony told me what y'all ordered, so I'm going to call the credit card company and just make sure that there are no charges for an order of the baby back ribs and spaghetti marinara. And some cheap red wine."

Jani spun around to face me. His breath smelled kind of ribby, come to think of it. "You've got no right, Bobbie," he snarled. "What about you and Vince, huh? I know all about it, so don't try denying."

"Oh, is that what Shannon told you? Well, let's find out!"

On my vanity table was our cordless phone. I grabbed it and dialed Sharise's number, my fingers trembling, and put the phone on loudspeaker.

"Hey, Sharise, so I'm here with Jani, and he wants to know if I have been having sex with your husband."

"What the fuck?" said Sharise.

"Yeah, put Vince on the phone, please." My voice was shaky.

"Sure, babe," said Sharise.

Jani's eyes were pleading with me to stop, but I was on a roll.

"Hey, Bobbie, it's Vince. What's up, honey?"

I told Vince to put the phone on loudspeaker so Sharise could hear.

"So I'm with Jani and he's wondering if you and I have been having sexual relations. I would like you to confirm that no, in fact, I have never once seen or touched your dick. Correct?"

"Yes, that is correct," said Vince, sounding confused.

"Okay, thanks, Vince. Now, one more question—how well do you know Shannon? Because she was making out with my husband tonight."

"Wait . . . Shannon, Robbie's girlfriend? I dunno, maybe you should ask Robbie, he's right here."

Jani's face turned from purple to deathly white.

"Oh, great, could you put Robbie on the line too?"

"What's going on?" I heard Robbie say in the background.

Sharise suggested we conference in Shannon, so that Robbie could ask her what was up.

"Great idea, Sharise," I said. Jani tried to grab the phone from me, but I pushed him away, furious.

"Okay, hold on," said Sharise. "What's Shannon's number, Robbie?"

Shannon's line rang.

"Hello?"

"Shannon, it's Robbie."

"Hey, baby! I just got home from the gym. What's cookin'?"

"Please tell me you are not sleeping with Jani Lane." Jani was having a small heart failure in the background. There was a pause at the other end.

"Wait, Jani? What, you think I'm desperate or something?"

"Well, I have it on good authority that you were just with him, Shannon, so stop lying."

"Robbie, just relax. I bet his wife is behind this. That bitch is crazy."

"Yup, you bet I am," I chimed in.

"Who is this?" said Shannon, confused.

"This is Bobbie Brown. I believe you had your tongue down my husband's throat earlier? Have a nice day."

I hung up the phone. Jani had already stormed out the front door. I didn't see him for three days, which was no surprise. Even though he never abused alcohol at home, Jani's drinking was becoming heavier as our marriage declined. He was drinking backstage, suffering blackouts and fits of anger. Jani's erratic behavior was about more than just us; he was a damaged man in the throes of an identity crisis. It was no longer "cool" to like hair rock. When Jani walked into the offices of his record label, Columbia, and noticed that a framed poster of Warrant had been replaced by one of grunge stars Alice in Chains, he saw the writing on the wall, literally. He was in no shape to save himself or his career, let alone our marriage.

Something I've noticed in all my male friends who have been musicians—it really affects them when their careers start to flag, even just a little. One minute everyone is kissing their ass, and when they start to slip, they don't know who to trust. That musical talent they have (often the only talent they have) is no longer in demand, and all the admiration disappears, especially from girls. The declining rock star starts feeling insecure and desperate, and very often, the result is that he turns into an über-whore, sleeping with everything that moves, just so he can feel like a rock star again, even just for the night. To this day, if a girlfriend tells me she is dating a musician and he is messing around, I try to explain it to them. *Anybody* who seeks that much adoration at all times, who needs *that* much attention, is going to have trouble with fidelity. Date a rock star, and you are almost 100 percent going to get hurt, because there are very few guys in that scene who are going to reject hot pussy, ever. Unless you can deal with that, or get your own thing going on the side, I say run for the hills.

MIAMI SNOWSTORM

The shock of discovering without a shadow of a doubt that my husband was cheating could have sent me in one of two directions. I could have stayed home and faced the music. Or I could have gone to Miami and done a mountain of cocaine. I chose the latter.

I got off the plane in Miami and headed straight for the house that had been rented by my modeling agency. I had been booked for several catalog and swimwear shoots, and Flame had hooked me up with a dope suite on the beach, as well as a shared house where all the models could hang out. I had told Jani that I still loved him but that I needed some space. I took Taylar to my mom's en route to Miami, where my girlfriend Jennifer Driver, also a model, was waiting. Jennifer was a five-foot-eleven blond knockout with legs forever who had just been on the cover of *Playboy*, in their "Women of South Beach" issue, and would later date Axl Rose. She and I hung out at the house for nearly two weeks, while I pretended not to think about my problems back in L.A.

My friend Jimmy Franzo, the guy who had forced my ex Kenny to get on a plane out of L.A. a few years ago, had reinvented himself as a Miami clubland honcho, and he co-owned the most happening spot in town, Velvet. It was a true South Beach bacchanal, a nocturnal carnival with drag queens and hot lesbians and go-go dancers, and a candlelit VIP area with blue walls, chandeliers, and velvet couches. That's where Jennifer and I found ourselves most nights, sipping champagne and putting the world to rights.

"So Tommy Lee is going to fly out and visit me tomorrow," said Jennifer, looking a little excited, but not very.

"Cool," I said, feeling like I needed another bump. *Miami coke is way better than L.A.'s,* I thought. "Wait, Tommy Lee from Mötley?"

"Yeah!"

"That's exciting, girl," I said, thinking back to being a teenager. "Tommy is so damn *cute!*"

Jennifer had been dating Tommy for a couple of weeks. He had seen her *Playboy* cover and contacted her agency to set up a date. Jennifer thought Tommy was okay, but she really liked the other guy she was seeing in Miami, a billionaire with a stake in the Anheuser-Busch Company. "I think he, like, owns Budweiser?" said Jennifer, innocently shrugging her shoulders. She really was drop-dead gorgeous, and I didn't blame her for playing the field. In fact, I felt old next to her. I was a mom, I was married, I had no dashing billionaires or Tommy Lees flying out to see me. Just one cheating husband, a head of freshly dyed black hair, and an eight ball of Miami's finest.

A couple of days later, Tommy arrived. Jennifer was busy working, or seeing the Budweiser guy, so she asked me to keep Tommy entertained.

"Your hair looks nice," said Tommy, peering over his sunglasses. We were eating lunch al fresco at some cute little Art Deco joint close to the beach.

Tommy and I had met a few times, out on the scene, but only very briefly. Tommy was always charming, but I'd never hung out with him one-on-one before. The fifteen-year-old inside me couldn't believe she was sitting across the table from the hottest rock star on the planet. But I wasn't about to let Tommy know that I had had a crush on him since high school. No way.

"So how's Jani?" he asked.

"Things are tough, but we're working on it," I said, forcing down some salad. I had just done a line in the bathroom and food was the last thing on my mind. "How's Mötley?"

"Oh, you know, we got rid of Vince. John Corabi's on vocals now. We're on hiatus before our tour, so I thought I'd come visit Jennifer."

"Jennifer's amazing, huh?"

"Yeah, she's cool. She's cool."

When Jennifer got home the three of us went out and partied at Velvet. I got ahold of more coke. I hadn't slept in a few days, so I figured I'd just finish the rest of this bag and then relax before my mom brought Taylar out to visit, later that week. But every time I started to come down from the blow, all I felt was panic. I obsessed over Jani's betrayal of me and our little family. I imagined him with Shannon, kissing her. I replayed the conversation on the phone. At least in the dim light of Velvet, unknown faces and bodies all around me, I could dance and forget my reality. My blurry Miami nights bled into one another until I had dissociated from reality almost completely, and by the time my mom and Taylar arrived to visit me, I was so agitated and confused I could barely string a sentence together.

"Bobbie, come out of the bathroom, or I'll call the police!" I had been in the shower for nearly two hours, sobbing hysterically, while my mom banged on the door. A few hours earlier, Taylar had banged her head on the side of a coffee table, and it had sent me into a tailspin. It was not a serious bang, but I should have been watching her more closely. "It's my fault!" I screamed. "I'm a drug addict, I'm on coke, I'm too high to be a mom!"

"Can I bring you a towel?"

"No! I'm ashamed! It's all my fault." I was shaking.

When I eventually emerged from the shower, my mom put me to bed and sat with me, Taylar on her knee, stroking my dark hair. "Don't carry on like that, Bobbie, you're going to get through this. We're all going to help you. Your hair looks terrible, by the way." I nodded, feeling calm for the first time since touching down in Miami.

My mom called Jani and told him that I was in a bad way, that she was going to bring me and Taylar home to Baton Rouge, and that I was going to go to rehab.

"No," said Jani.

"What?"

"I don't think that's a good idea."

"That boy doesn't have a grain of sense," said my mom, hanging up the phone.

My mom was baffled as to why Jani would be against my going to rehab. I think deep down, Jani knew that the second I got sober, he would lose me forever.

DOING THE BATON ROUGE TWELVE-STEP

My mom flew me and Taylar home to Baton Rouge, and Mr. Earl called SAG, the Screen Actors Guild, which agreed to pay for me to go to a local outpatient rehab for six weeks.

"Bobbie, you're gonna stay here and rest," said Mr. Earl. Then he called to my mom, "I'm going to the store, honey. Bobbie is all skin and bones."

Being a fast-talking cocaine addict from Los Angeles, it was hard for me to adjust to Southern life again. The addicts in my twelve-step group, especially, spoke so damn slow it took half an hour for them just to say their names.

"Hi, mah naaaame is Patty Mae, and ahm an allllllco-haaaaaalic."

I had never been to an AA meeting before, but it seemed like everyone in rural Louisiana had taken up smoking crack since I had left.

"So how was everybody's weeeeekend?" asked the therapist.

"I went for a drive," said a wiry balding crackhead called Elijah, sweat dripping down his temples. "And then I lost mah keys. So I looked for mah keys. And I said, 'Well, darn. I can't find mah keys.'"

"Dude, who gives a fuck!" I blurted. "Did you use or not?"

"All right now, shugah, hush yo' mouth," said the doctor, and the group tutted and shook their heads. "Bobbie's ill as a hornet this mornin'," said the doctor, giving me a sympathetic smile.

I couldn't believe I was in the company of actual crackheads. What with my being a glamorous model/actress coke addict.

"Honey, you realize you talk about your husband nonstop?" said Elijah. "I think y'all are havin' a toxic relationship over there."

"Yes, everthang's awl messed up with y'all," said Twyla Fay, junkie and mother of three. "What about *you*, Bobbie? What do *you* want? You're a fahn-lookin' woman."

"Yup, mighty fetchin'," added Elijah.

The crackheads had a point. I didn't really know what I wanted. Not since leaving Louisiana to become a model had I thought about what I really wanted out of life, in the long term.

"Well, I want to be a good momma," I said, slowly. "I want to be happy. And I don't want liars in my life."

The more time I spent in group therapy, the more I realized it would be impossible for me to achieve those things within my marriage to Jani. Especially now, with all the rumors I was hearing, how in my absence Jani was drinking heavily and up to no good. How he was seeing this girl or that girl; how he was bringing them back to our home. I called Jani, pissed. "I am not going to be in this marriage if you are fucking other bitches, you understand?"

Jani denied everything and flew out to see me in Baton Rouge in a desperate bid to save our marriage. My mom and Mr. Earl made themselves scarce while Jani and I talked it out in my bedroom. "Your stories keep changing, Jani," I yelled. "Can you just be completely honest with me for once?" I just wanted the truth. Finally, Jani told me what I already knew. There wasn't just one woman—there had been many. Jani was a serial cheater.

"Anytime I was with anybody else, I was always loving you, Bobbie," he pleaded. "I was just selfish and insecure, and they were giving me attention. I'm so sorry. Please, let's work this out." Jani's heart was breaking in front of me. But a sickness took over my whole body, and I started shaking. "Fuck that shit," I said. "If you love someone, you don't fuck other people and lie about it!" It didn't make any sense to me back then. "Get your shit, pack your bag, and get the fuck out of here." Then I ran into the bathroom and threw up.

I remember how confident I was when Jani and I first fell

in love. How I never ever thought he would cheat on me. Even when Joan Rivers asked me, on her show, "Aren't you concerned about marrying a rock star? Once a playboy, always a playboy."

What a bitch, I thought.

"No way would Jani cheat on me. Not in a million years," I told her, indignant.

Back in group therapy, my fellow addicts tried to help me understand that Jani's cheating was not about me. It was about his insecurity. But it's really hard not to take cheating personally, especially when you are married. I was getting calls from Jani's mom. "Bobbie, Jani had a breakdown, he's in the hospital, saying you want to divorce him and he can't handle it. Please, can you give him another chance? He loves you." But I couldn't do it. I wasn't strong enough to take him back. He was supposed to be the guy I could rely on. The one who loved me the most. The Cherry Pie boy and the Cherry Pie girl were supposed to be together forever. He had fucked it up, as far as I was concerned. "So I'm supposed to forgive and forget now just because he's in the hospital? I already gave him a second chance. I'm still young; I can still find a partner who I can at least trust."

Three months after I came back from rehab, we officially separated. Jani fell into yet another tailspin, clinging to the people and the habits that were bad for him. I wish I could have stayed with Jani, but I couldn't get past the lies. Sober, and with my eyes wide open, I filed for divorce.

PRINCE CHARMING ON A HARLEY

"Hey, it's Tommy Lee, your Miami buddy. You and Jani should come over to my place sometime. Miss you!"

Tommy Lee had been calling the house. I hadn't had the time or mental capacity to get back to him—I was in the middle of restructuring my entire life and preparing to become a single mother, now that my marriage was ending. My mother flew to California and took Taylar back with her to Baton Rouge for a little while so that I could regroup. Being alone felt surreal. I was sober. I was single. I had a strange, raw clarity. My life was at ground zero and I was starting over, divorced in Hollywood at the age of twenty-four. The next time I fell in love, I told myself, it would be with someone completely different. Someone stronger, less insecure.

Once word got out that Jani and I were splitting, the hair metal hounds came sniffing. "So Bret Michaels hit on me—*while he was on a date*," I told Sharise on the phone. I couldn't believe how the men in this scene behaved, not just toward women, but toward each other. They seemed to have so little loyalty toward one another.

"Ew, really?" said Sharise.

"Yeah, he sent his bodyguard to tell me to meet him in the kitchen of the restaurant, so I did, and then he asked me out. And I was like, 'But what about your date out there?'"

"What a dork!"

"I know. Talk about tacky!"

Sharise was my biggest supporter. She too was going

through her own problems, and she would divorce Vince Neil the same year I divorced Jani. Sharise and I have led parallel lives in that way. While Jani was quitting and then getting back into Warrant, Vince was getting fired from Mötley Crüe. Sharise and I were both mothers, and Sharise's little girl, Skylar, was the center of her world. Sharise and I talked almost every day, and she was anxious that I start moving on from Jani as soon as possible.

"You know, it might be too soon, but I do know someone who is dying to see you, Bobbie. And it isn't Bret Michaels."

"Who?" I asked, curious.

"Tommy. He's saying he's in love with you."

Now this was an unexpected turn of events. Had it been anyone else in the world, any other rocker in Hollywood, I would have said forget it. But *Tommy Lee*, my teenage crush, my Prince Charming on a Harley? I had been planning on taking some time out before even contemplating dating. But for Tommy, maybe, I would make an exception.

I was at Club Ugly, a club night that Sharise had started at a venue called the Dragonfly in Hollywood. It was *the* place to be on a Thursday night. Everyone who was anyone was there. Johnny Depp came in one night and ended up getting together with Sharise. ("He's into clowns," she told me the next day. "Creepy!") Danny Boy from House of Pain, and my dance buddy Jay Gordon were regulars. Now that I had separated from Jani, Jay was all up in my grill, but I was not down.

"Sex changes everything, and I don't want things to get weird between us!" I told Jay on the dance floor. "You're wrong, sex will make our friendship even better," he yelled back. "Listen, Jay, stick around long enough, and I might cave in," I conceded. "But you'll probably be waiting a long time!"

"Nice chaps, Bobbie Brown!" I turned around to face Tommy Lee, who had snuck up behind me. Yes, I was wearing chaps, with a leotard underneath. It was a hot look back then. And Tommy seemed to appreciate it. He said he wanted to sit down and talk. He told me how he had broken up with Jennifer months ago. I told him how Jani and I were over and how it was for the best. We talked about how we are both Libras—his birthday is on the third of October and mine is on the seventh. We talked until the club shut down.

I was driving home when my cell phone rang. It was Tommy. We had said good-bye outside the club not five minutes ago.

"Hey, Tommy, what's up?"

"I just wanted to tell you you're the fucking shit; you're the hottest woman in the world. I'm screaming it out my car window, right now."

And he was. I heard him screaming my name, yelling how hot Bobbie Brown was.

Then he came back on the line.

"Bobbie, I'm going to go home and jerk off while I think about you."

Whoa. Tommy wasn't playing coy. Later that night, my phone rang again. It was Tommy.

"Bobbie!" he groaned.

"Tommy, are you okay?"

"I'm coming!" I heard groans as Tommy Lee shot his load. "Oh fuck yeah, I just came."

I hung up the phone. *What the fuck?* Tommy was the nuttiest guy I had ever met.

Tommy started sending me flowers. Huge bouquets, a different one each day. My girlfriend Annie came over for lunch and was startled to see so many roses and irises and orchids everywhere. "Who died?" she said, wading through them. "Wait, these are from *Tommy*? Ooooh, the plot thickens. Tommy, Jani, Tommy, Jani . . . which one will she pick?"

"Shut up, dude."

That night, Tommy called—he wanted to take me out for dinner. I said okay, still a little unsure about how to deal with his dramatic gestures of appreciation. He showed up in his red Ferrari and flashed me that smile . . . Tommy had it going on, and he knew it. He was hard to resist. We went to a Greek restaurant, threw dishes in the fireplace, and laughed our asses off, as usual. The restaurant had a rooftop garden, so after dinner we stood out there in the wind and took in the views. The Santa Anas were blowing, hot winds that the Spanish call "devil's breath" or "murder winds."

"I dare you to rip your shirt open in the wind," said Tommy as we leaned off the railing of the restaurant roof. My hair whipped about my face. I tore my shirt open, and all the buttons popped off. I closed my eyes and flung my arms out. "Shit, your tits are huge!" Tommy exclaimed. I wasn't on coke, I wasn't drunk, I wasn't thinking about Jani. For the first time in years, I felt free. The last thing I needed was to get wrapped up in some guy . . . but I didn't want to stop seeing Tommy. We had just too strong a connection for me to let it die; I just had to figure out a way to stay in control of the situation, to not let myself fall in love.

Each time we went on a date, I would bring a cockblocker, a girlfriend whose job it was to make sure Tommy and I were never alone together. The only man I had been with in the last three years was Jani Lane, and the thought of jumping into bed with crazy Tommy Lee was just way too scary. "Dude, am I fucking ugly or something?" Tommy asked a mutual friend. "Bobbie won't even make out with me!" Despite my apparent lack of interest, Tommy was undeterred. He asked if he could stay the night at my house, and curled on the floor by my bed. "I just want to breathe your air, Bobbie," he said. "Okay whatever," I said, brushing my teeth and putting on my pajamas. In the morning, there he was, still on the floor. I told him he could shower if he liked, and when he emerged, skin glistening, a teeny white towel wrapped around his hips, I had to turn away. *Sweet baby Jesus. Be strong, Bobbie Brown, be strong!*

Hot as he was, I tried to remind myself of the very good reasons why I should not get romantically involved with him. Namely:

1. Tommy's a hound. There were countless strippers, whores, and Hollywood sluts who had been acquainted with Tommy's assets (video babe Tawny Kitaen, porn star Debi Diamond, even

Cher, for Christ's sake). Being married (to Heather Locklear, from 1986 to 1993) had never seemed to hold him back.

2. Tommy had to be an STD factory (see previous entry).

3. Tommy was probably into some crazy shit in the bedroom, and Bobbie Brown was done working hard for the dick. No more showboating.

I was out of practice, undersexed, and overwhelmed. But Tommy Lee gets what Tommy Lee wants. It was just a matter of time. "Come sit down next to me," Tommy said, patting the couch one night at my house. It was late 1993, and we had been "just good friends" for nearly four months. I sat down—at the opposite end of the couch. He edged closer to me. I made to stand, and he pulled me back down. "Goddammit, Bobbie!"

He kissed me, but after a minute or so, I pulled back. Tommy sighed, exasperated. "You must think I'm fucking ugly or something," he said, shaking his head. "What the fuck? And why is it you always bring a cockblocker every time we go out?" I took a deep breath. "Tommy, it's just . . . you're Tommy Lee. I've been crushing on you since high school."

"Seriously?"

"I'm scared. I don't know if I'm going to be able to please you. I'm just some dork." Tommy's brow furrowed. "You're silly. I'm so attracted to you. I want you so much. And trust me, you don't have to do anything crazy. Just be you."

Tommy started kissing me slowly. The kiss built into something more passionate. Slowly, he undressed me, stroking my skin lightly. I started babbling, revealing my hand. "I've been crushing on you for, like, ever, Tommy. I think I gave myself my first orgasm looking at a Mötley Crüe poster."

"I love you, Bobbie." I wasn't expecting that. Immediately I grew suspicious.

"Fuck you!"

"No. I really do."

He led my hand down below. *Dear God, it's like a baby's arm.*

"Holy shit, Tommy . . . I think I love you too."

Kissing Tommy felt surreal. Was this really happening, or was I just a teenager again, having a dream? I felt nervous, unsure of myself. Was he going to bite me all over? Did he want to slap me? Did I have to slap him? Was he going to bust out some nipple clamps and candle wax? But it wasn't freaky. We had normal, missionary-position sex with him kissing me the whole time and looking in my eyes. "You're so beautiful. You're so amazing." He was flattering the shit out of me. "Look at your teeth—my God, you have the most amazing teeth. I just want to eat your face."

"Shut up." I never was good at accepting compliments. Afterward, I lay in his arms, seeing stars. "Bobbie, I think you and Taylar should move in with me," said Tommy. "I want to be with you every day. Please think about it."

It was game on.

And the way we expressed our love was with our bodies. Our chemistry was off the charts. We had sex at least three times a day, and we craved each other every second we were apart. The exact opposite of how things had been with Jani.

One morning Tommy and I were in bed, when we heard banging on the door. Tommy got up and went to the front door, towel wrapped around him, cigarette hanging from his lip.

"You're doing my wife!" screamed Jani, standing on the doorstep. "In my *house*? Who do you think you are?"

"Jani, c'mon, you guys are over. What's your problem?" said Tommy, keeping his cool.

Jani got up in his face.

"So how do I taste, asshole? Because each time you eat her pussy, that's my dick you're tasting."

"How do you *taste*?" Tommy licked his lips and thought about it. "Actually . . . delicious."

Jani stormed off, horrified. For the rest of that day, he bombarded Tommy's cell phone with calls and messages. Eventually Tommy picked up.

"How could you date my wife? I thought we were friends, Tommy."

"Well, if she didn't insist on fucking me until my dick was sore, it might be easier to leave." Tommy was the perfect asshole and his crass bragging hit Jani right where it hurt: his ego.

"You're evil, Tommy," said Jani.

Right after that, Jani changed his voice mail message to a sample of a Beck song. "I'm a loser baby . . . so why don't you kill me." It broke my heart every time I heard it. But I was in deep with Tommy. There was no going back.

Even after Jani and I divorced in 1993, Jani constantly tried to win me back. His attempts to seduce me always fell flat, though. I would go to his house to pick up child support, for instance, and he would open the door butt naked and scamper to the bedroom, assuming, for some reason, that I would follow him. But I was no longer the needy Bobbie who begged Jani for attention. I had moved on. "Where did you go?" he would say, calling me later. "I went away, Jani. You know that." Life with Tommy was so easy, I couldn't believe I had ever put myself through the strain of being married to Jani Lane.

Everything with Tommy was hilarious. It was nonstop jokes. Which of course made me love him even more, because if you can make me laugh, that is eternal. Jani had always *thought* he was funny, but his humor had been dorky to me. Tommy's humor was sharp, though, really hilarious. We laughed so much, we had to figure out a way to kiss and laugh at the same time, seeing as those were the two things we seemed to do most. He would grab my face while we were cracking up and start kissing me while our mouths were open. Sounds gross, but it was cute. Maybe you had to be there. Either way, it looked kind of similar to what Tommy would be photographed doing with Pamela Anderson, not too long after.

Tommy, like all the rock guys I had been with, would fly me out to meet him on the road at any given opportunity. One time, we were at an airport newsstand, and Tommy got all excited. "Hey, babe, I didn't know you'd done *Playboy*?" He was holding up a copy of that month's issue. "What are you talking about?" I said, peering at it. "Dude, are you serious?" It was Pamela

Anderson on the cover—not me. He looked more closely. "Oh, shit, babe, I'm sorry. You guys look kinda similar."

"You really think so, huh?"

"Babe, I just made a mistake. I think she looks like RuPaul, anyway. What's up with her eyebrows?"

"So now you're saying I look like RuPaul. Great." Sometimes Tommy was his own worst enemy.

WARNING SIGNS

They say that when it comes to abusive men, the signs are usually there from the get-go. The hard part is accepting it. Tommy and I were at the Roxbury, and I could not believe what I was seeing: he had Sharise's brother Gary by the throat, pinned down to a table.

"Don't talk to my fucking woman!" This was some caveman shit.

"Tommy, let him go! That's Sharise's brother!"

Tommy looked at me with wild, jealous eyes.

"What are you, a fucking whore?"

As soon as we started sleeping together, I became property of Tommy Lee, like it or not. He wanted me with him all day and all night, and any motherfucker with a penis who dared come within a mile of me better watch his back. Even my friend-zone boyfriends had taken note of Tommy's possessiveness and were keeping their distance. But how was Sharise's brother to know?

Tommy was starting to remind me of my father, the way he would trip out without any warning.

In the limo on our way back to his place, I told Tommy I was having doubts about moving in. "You really flipped the fuck out back there. That's some loony tunes shit, you know that, right? I have a daughter, Tommy, I can't be taking any chances." Tommy said that he loved me and swore that it would never happen again. Ah, those famous last words.

THE DAY THE EARTH MOVED

"Holy shiiiiit!"

There was a huge boom, as though God was pounding the biggest kick drum in the universe. Then it felt like someone had picked up the house and was shaking it. Books and furniture flew through the air. Water cascaded as our pool cracked and its contents drained into the neighbor's yard. There was a terrible creak as the kitchen separated from the living room.

The Northridge earthquake occurred at 4:30 A.M. on January 17, 1994. A magnitude 6.7 quake, it was the largest and costliest natural disaster in United States history, killing nearly sixty people and causing more than $40 billion in damages.

When it happened, Tommy and I were crashed out on the floor of my bedroom in my house in Tarzana, about seven miles from the epicenter. I had just had my boobs redone.

"It's fucking Armageddon," I screamed, clinging to Tommy.

Tommy and I were sleeping on the floor because my surgery had made it too painful for me to climb up the ladder to my high, loft-style bed. I heard my mom screaming down the hall—she was in town to help me out after my surgery. But she hadn't bargained on this.

"What the fuck was that?" said my mother, who never curses. She was holding Taylar, who was grinning like a kid on a roller coaster. "Wheeee!" said Taylar as the house continued to rock and tremble.

"That was an earthquake, Mom, a big one! Welcome to Los Angeles."

"That's it—I'm never coming back to this fucking town," said my mom, cursing for the second time in her life.

The four of us sat in the car in my driveway for several hours, afraid to go back inside because the aftershocks were so huge. We had no idea what was going to happen to the house, the city, even the state. All the power was out everywhere, and people were freaking out, tripping balls. "Mom, take Taylar back with you." We couldn't stay at my house anymore, so Tommy and I booked ourselves in at a hotel in nearby Woodland Hills. The house, which Jani and I had bought just before we split, had never really felt like home anyway. I started spending all my time at Tommy's place, and he started looking for a home for us on the beach. It felt like the universe was conspiring for us to be together.

My mom took Taylar back to Baton Rouge with her for a few

months while I dealt with the aftermath. It was not the first time she would take over parenting duties for me, and would not be the last. Whether it was earthquakes, heartbreak, or drug addiction, my mother, Judy Ann, would always be there for me and my daughter—holding our hands, reassuring us that everything would work out in the end. And now that I'd found Tommy, even she believed that I might have gotten a second chance at happiness with a rock star.

Chapter Eight

HE'S MY TOMMY LEE

There are all kinds of stories out there about how Tommy Lee met Pamela Anderson. Some say they met at a New Year's party while he was high on ecstasy. Some say they met when Tommy licked her face at a club. The truth is, I introduced them. Sharise, Tommy, and I were at Bar One, a club on the Sunset Strip near Beverly Hills that Vince Neil had part ownership of and occasionally rented out for porn shoots. Pamela was at a table with an acquaintance of mine, a club promoter named Billy Atkins. The three of us were passing through the crowd, and Billy grabbed my arm. "Hey, Bobbie, you know Pam?"

"Of course. Hello, Pam." They invited us to sit down at their booth and have some cocktails. "So aren't you going to introduce me to your guy, Bobbie?" said Pamela, looking at Tommy. "I've been dying to meet you."

"Tommy, this is Pamela Anderson. Pamela, meet Tommy Lee."

I didn't think anything of it. Pamela and I had known each other for a few years, from working on *Married . . . with Children* and seeing each other around Hollywood. Now she was famous as C. J. Parker on *Baywatch*, which had become the highest-rated TV program in the world, thanks, largely, to her. Magazines had been comparing the two of us, sometimes calling me "the new Pamela Anderson." Yes, we had a similar look—tousled blond hair, sexy pout, silicone tits. We weren't twins, though. With my motor mouth and down-home attitude, I was all slacker meets Valley girl, whereas Pamela had that white-trash Brigitte Bardot thing going on. Our personalities, especially, were very different. Pamela was coy and always played her cards close to her giant chest. I wore my heart on my sleeve and was incapable of doing "cute." I was the goofball tomboy to Pamela's aloof vixen.

We had already had some professional run-ins—back when I was with Jani, Hugh Hefner had offered me a *Playboy* pictorial and I arrived on set only to find that they had canceled the shoot at the last minute, for "political" reasons. I caught wind that Pamela, who had been on four covers, was not happy about her doppelgänger Bobbie Brown inching onto her turf. But I wasn't one to hold on to a grudge.

"Tommy, so good to meet you finally!" said Pamela, a half smile playing on her freshly glossed lips. Pamela started talking about herself, how she ate organic and cared about the environment and only used a little bit of electricity compared to her neighbors. "Also, I can play the drums," she added, playing air drums and shaking her hair, and Tommy nodded, impressed. Sharise turned to me, mouthing, "What the fuck?"

"So I'm dating David Charvet, this guy on my show *Baywatch*," Pamela continued, eyes fixed on Tommy's. "Talk about a pencil dick. I'm so over it!" (They dated for about two years and then Charvet went on to marry Brooke Burke, cohost of *Dancing with the Stars*, which Pamela became a contestant on.) "That sucks," said Tommy, looking amused. "Where I come from, they throw the small ones back." We all laughed, and Tommy squeezed my hand reassuringly. But something didn't feel right.

What is up with Pamela tonight? I wondered. She was trying a little too hard. I knew she was a big fan of rock music, so maybe she was just nervous. She hung on Tommy's every word. It was obvious she had no interest in what anyone else had to say—her conversation was directed solely toward him. She had a reputation for being a guy's girl, one whose identity revolved around men's attention. She had few female friends in Hollywood, and it was pretty obvious what her goal was in town—to make it. My professional ambition, on the other hand, had been stymied by love, motherhood, and the pursuit of fun.

We sat with them for about forty-five minutes; then, when Tommy said he wanted to go to the Viper Room, Pamela invited herself along with us. At the Viper Room, Sharise and I got onstage and started dancing, and Pamela joined us, gyrating and shaking her tits all over the place. It was amazingly awkward for Sharise and me, because not only were we unused to having a third wheel, we also knew she wasn't really trying to be our friend—it felt like she was trying to show off in front of Tommy. That much was obvious. Carmen Electra was at one of the tables next to the stage, and when she yelled up at us saying she wanted to dance too, I was relieved—as soon as Carmen jumped up, Sharise and I jumped down off the stage, leaving them to it.

"Hey, my brother just texted saying the doorman won't let him in," said Sharise. I told Tommy, who said, "No problem, let me go and talk to the bouncer." He grabbed Sharise's hand and the two of them marched outside to make sure her brother could get in. Pamela, who had been watching, sidled up to me. "What's up with homegirl holding your boyfriend's hand? I wouldn't stand for that shit." I was stunned. Why was Pamela planting thoughts like that in my head? "Hey, it's no big deal—Sharise is my best friend, and they are like brother and sister." When Sharise came back, I told her what Pamela had said. "Fuck *her*!" said Sharise. "What a weirdo!"

It wasn't the first time I had seen a woman try to sabotage my relationship with Tommy. But I told myself not to worry about it. Tommy and I had a love that was unbreakable, immune to the advances of *all* women—even Pamela Anderson.

TOMMY'S GIRL

I had, against my better judgment, moved in with Tommy by this point. He had rented actress Sela Ward's three-bedroom love nest on the beach in Malibu Colony, and Taylar and our nanny, Gretchen (Taylar called her "Scratchin'"), Tommy, and I were living there in glorious beachfront decadence.

One afternoon, Tommy and I were shopping for furniture

and my eyes rested on a beautiful ornate bed. It looked like the carriage in *Cinderella*.

"Is that the one you want?" said Tommy.

"It's a total fairy-tale bed," I gushed.

"It's ours," he said, and wrote a check for fifteen thousand dollars on the spot.

I had never seen anyone drop $15K on a whim like that. Jani and I had owned a nice home, and I made good money modeling, but we weren't crazy rich like Mötley Crüe. Mötley Crüe had a plane, for God's sake. Our rent in Malibu was eight thousand dollars a month. We had four cars. Tommy bought Ferraris and motorcycles when he felt like it. Once, he bought me ten-thousand-dollar leather pants. Now I look back on that, and I think it was dumb. But it was 1994. The recession of the early '90s was over, and America was feeling prosperous. *Beavis and Butthead* was the most intelligent thing on TV. The Wonderbra was a feminist statement—it was a fun, foolish time to be American.

Tommy didn't want me to work. His ex-wife Heather Locklear had been all about her career, and he'd hated not being the center of her attention. He never said anything bad about Heather, just that their problems arose from her being more invested in her acting than in the relationship. He said he wanted a woman who was about him, who wasn't trying to be in the limelight. "I am *so* not into paparazzi and being in the public eye anymore—it's *so* cheesy," he would say. He insisted that I quit modeling for a while and promised to take care of me in return. I didn't need to make money—I was Tommy's girl.

Taylar, now two years old, called him "Dad Tommy." He loved to have fun with her, although I would stop short of calling him paternal. Tommy is a big kid, which is why children always love being around him, but he also behaved like a big kid when he wanted attention. And he had no qualms about competing for that attention, even with a small child. Sometimes, for instance, I would hear my daughter cry and start to get up to see what was wrong, and Tommy would pull me back.

"Don't get up. Stay here with me."

"Of course I'm getting up," I would say, pulling away.

I had become friends with Athena, Tommy's younger sister. Athena was in a punk group called Butt Trumpet and had a daughter, Tobi, who was a little older than Taylar, and a two-year-old boy called Miles. She was a monster on the drums, having taught herself to play in the soundproof garage Tommy's dad had built, honing her skills on Tommy's *Theatre of Pain* kit. When Tommy was on the road, Athena and I would hang out at the house in Malibu, giggling at the many faxes Tommy loved to send me from the road, saying how much he missed me. Yeah, love faxes—that's how '90s we were. When Tommy would roll home, whoever was at the house would take a hike. Because with Tommy and me, it was zero to naked in sixty seconds. I have never experienced such insane sexual chemistry as I had with Tommy Lee.

ENJOY THE FEELING AS THE BALLS PASS THROUGH

"What if I do it slowly and maybe work it in?" said Tommy, trying to coax me into anal. The only other time I had had anal sex was with Jani, when he tied me up. That experience had freaked me out, so I was wary of letting anyone back there again. Tommy promised to be gentle, but it really didn't work out the way he had hoped. "Wait . . . stop . . . fuck that, your dick's too big, Tommy! Ouch! Get it away from my ass!"

He bought me a vibrator that had a rabbit on the end and a little tongue. It was loud as a lawn mower. You could hear it on the other side of the house. *Waaaaaaah.* And it had two settings—intense, and fucking intense. "Dude, that thing was ripping me apart!" I told Tommy, handing it back to him in the box. "Did you keep the receipt?" For a rock star's girlfriend, I was pretty vanilla I guess, but that's just me. I wasn't ashamed of it.

"How about we try these instead?" he said, going into the bathroom and coming out with a box. Inside was a string of little purple balls of increasing size. "What is this, a jump rope?" I read the side of the packaging. "'Insert through the anus into the rectum, and at the point of climax, pull out and enjoy the feeling as the balls pass through your sphincter.'" Ah.

"I guess they were all out of the starter kits, huh, Tommy?" There were six beads, listed as "medium to large size." I wished he could have at least gotten them in "small."

"How about we shove these up your ass first, and then if you like it, I'll give them a go afterward," I said. Tommy turned up his nose. "Oh, forget it."

The way I saw it, we didn't need anal beads or girl-on-girl porn or dildos or anything beyond each other's bodies, really. Sex with Tommy was always great, because I was so in love. Of course, it didn't hurt that he had a big dick—although all that really means is that the guy doesn't have to work very hard. When you're really into somebody, sex is special, regardless of his length, girth, or the number of sex toys next to the bed.

I WANNA WIFE YOU

In the summer of 1994, around six months into our relationship, I flew out to meet Tommy on tour in the Midwest. He had a limo pick me up from the airport and suggested we drive straight back to the Four Seasons, where he was staying, so we could have dinner in the fancy French restaurant there. He could have taken me to Chuck E. Cheese's for all I cared. I just wanted to see him.

Tommy waved at the waiter. "Can you bring over that dessert we were talking about?" When the waiter returned, he was holding a ring case, which he handed to Tommy. Tommy pushed it across the table to me—inside was a four-carat diamond ring set in platinum, with diamonds on the side.

"I wanna wife you, Bobbie," he said.

"Oh my God!" I gasped, tears welling in my eyes.

I was twenty-five years old, with one rock star divorce under my belt. He was thirty-two, with two ex-wives under his. The first was a Canadian dancer/stripper named Elaine Bergen, in 1984. She was a dancer at the Body Shop, a titty bar on the Sunset Strip, and her stripper name was Candice Starrek. A sultry brunette, she did a spread in *Penthouse*, which is where she caught Tommy's eye (*Playboy* and *Penthouse* were basically like the Match.com for models and rock stars back then). That marriage lasted a whole month, until she supposedly tried to stab him with a butter knife and he punched her in the mouth, knocking a cap off her tooth.

Then he pulled a 180 and got with fresh-faced blond actress Heather Locklear, who was famous for playing the bitchy Sammy Jo on popular nighttime soap *Dynasty* and Amanda on *Melrose Place*. Tommy had spotted her backstage at an REO Speedwagon concert at L.A.'s Forum. Then he stalked her through her dentist. Three months after they started dating, she proposed to him in a Texas hotel room. Tommy walked up the aisle chewing gum, wearing a white leather tux. They were married from 1986 to 1993, and had divorced shortly before we got together. Tommy, I would later realize, is a compulsive proposer. He's been engaged many, many times. Tommy Lee just does not like to be single.

Shortly after we became engaged, Tommy tattooed my name in cursive script along his neck. Years later, he told me that having that tattoo removed was more painful than any ink work he had ever received. All that was yet to come.

MALIBU MAYHEM

One thing about Tommy, he hated clothes. Clothes on me, specifically. I wasn't allowed to sleep in pajamas, ever. If Bobbie wasn't naked, Tommy wasn't happy. I would be cleaning up or doing dishes, and he'd yell at me, "Come sit next to me, fuck the dishes."

"But I want to do the dishes, Tommy."

"Take your clothes off and come sit next to me!" He was like a spoiled little boy.

"I don't want to be naked watching TV, Tommy, *I want to do the fucking dishes!*"

Sometimes I felt like a big doll. He wanted to take out my tampons; he wanted to shave my legs. If he could have crawled inside me, he would have. It was strange to me that someone with so much success in his life would be so needy and codependent. "Where were you, what were you doing?" Tommy would ask me if I left him alone for more than a few minutes.

"Um, I went to go take a shit." It was annoying. He was like a neurotic five-year-old.

Boom!

A huge explosion came from the beach. It must have woken up the whole of Malibu. And this time, it wasn't an earthquake.

Tommy came running into the house, half his eyebrow and half of his shirt smoldering. "Okay, I guess that wasn't a cherry bomb," he said, laughing maniacally. "Close the storm windows, let's hide!" When Tommy wasn't playing with my boobs, he was blowing shit up. Like I say, it was like living with a big out-of-control kid.

Those first few months in Malibu were all fun and games. Our friends would come over to party all night and hang out on the beach. I was, by now, fully off the wagon, although my partying wasn't worrying me. It felt recreational, I told myself. And my daughter was never exposed to any of it. There were always people coming and going through the house, new friends, old friends, and sycophants by the truckload. Elijah Blue, Cher's son. Whitfield Crane of Ugly Kid Joe. Matt Sorum from Guns N' Roses. Bobby Hewitt, the drummer of Orgy. Athena and her new guy James Kottak from the Scorpions. Because Malibu is waaay up the coast from Hollywood, far from everybody and everything, people would come and stay at our place for days on end. Each day blended into the next as life became one long Malibu beach party.

Anybody who looked up to Tommy would become his new best friend, because he, like so many musicians, thrives on adoration. Elijah Blue, for example, lived down the street at Cher's place and thought Tommy was the coolest thing in the world, which Tommy liked. Elijah had been making music, and Tommy invited him to play some for us. "That's the shit; that's awesome!" said Tommy. *Hm, I'm not so sure,* I thought, but I kept my mouth shut. Tommy hated it when I contradicted him in front of people. In fact, Tommy hated a lot of things, but it was easy to ignore his bratty side, because when he was in a good mood, he was awesome. Tommy was wild, he was funny, he was the only man whose mouth could keep up with mine. He put me so high on a pedestal that I could barely see the ground anymore. Then, before I knew it, he was yanking me down by my hair. It was the blow I should have seen coming, but refused to.

One night, Mötley was playing in L.A. and I was chatting with Nikki Sixx's gorgeous wife Brandi Brandt, side-stage. Brandi was even-keeled and soft spoken. I glanced at the stage mid-conversation and saw that Tommy was looking at me with these crazy eyes as he drummed.

"Uh-oh, I think I'm in trouble," I said to Brandi.

"Why are you in trouble?" said Brandi softly.

"I'm not sure."

Sure enough, after the show, Tommy tore me a new asshole. "What the fuck, Bobbie, this isn't social hour. You are here to see *me*. What, you don't fucking love me anymore?" Tommy was becoming more and more of a brat by the day. I couldn't go anywhere without him. I couldn't hang out alone with my friends or Tommy would get jealous. He had to be a part of everything I did unless he was on tour, in which case I had to go see him whenever possible. If I hung out with friends, it had to be at our home. He was uncomfortable with how close I was getting to Athena. He didn't even like my talking to my mom too much, so he got a phone service to field all calls to the house. He started criticizing my appearance. If I didn't have makeup on, he would get mad, saying, "What, you're not trying to get with me?" And if I was dolled up, he would be like, "Who are you trying to fuck?"

I had gained a little weight from playing the wife role, cooking and hanging out and basically being Tommy's girl for a living. I would prepare him three solid meals a day—lasagna, homemade potpies, the works. His favorite thing was Cajun sausage and scrambled eggs for breakfast. Although he loved my food, he didn't love my new fuller figure. I called a friend in the modeling business. "I need something to help me get thin again," I said. Less than twenty-four hours later, I was holding a small bag of crystal meth in my hand.

I sat in our bedroom, with a dish on my lap, and cut the powder with one of Tommy's credit cards. I had heard you didn't need that much speed to feel the effects, so I made a very small line. The first hit was a surprise. Unlike cocaine, it burned, sending lightning bolts through my eyeballs. I learned to look past the pain, because this was a high like no other. It felt . . . natural. My ADD mind felt oddly at peace. One of the chief things meth does is to release serotonin in the brain, so suddenly I was the optimistic, positive, confident Bobbie again. Plus, I could cook dinner for Tommy without the tiniest urge to taste what was in the pan. From day one, I was hooked.

The weekend I started using speed (behind Tommy's back, for the record), Tommy took us out on his boat to Lake Mead near Las Vegas for a mini vacation (you might recognize the location from the sex tape he and Pamela Anderson would make, in the not too distant future). I didn't eat anything the whole weekend, because the speed I had taken had, to my glee, completely destroyed my appetite. "Why aren't you eating?" Tommy asked me, and I told him I just didn't feel hungry, no biggie. Tommy wanted me to water-ski, which I had never tried before, but when I tried to get up, my legs buckled beneath me. I was too weak for water sports. My body was starving. I could practically feel the weight dropping off as my metabolism sped up . . . I liked it.

From day one, I started using a little speed every day, and was impressed at how quickly I was losing weight. Very soon it got to the point where I was *too* thin. Grotesquely thin. There is a photo I did for *Cosmopolitan* (one of the rare modeling gigs I did during that period) in which I weighed ninety pounds. Now, instead of making fun of my curves, Tommy was calling me Skeletor. I couldn't win. But I had given up everything, handed Tommy complete power and control over me. The more I gave up, the less he respected me. The less he respected me, the more I used. The more I used, the less I respected myself. The cycle of addiction had begun. I was starting to fuck up big-time, throwing away opportunities that could have made me a major star, because my life's focus had now narrowed to just two things—Tommy and drugs.

Robert De Niro called the house, trying to convince Tommy to let me read for the part of Ginger, his wife in the movie *Casino*, with Martin Scorsese set to direct. The mighty Robert De Niro was calling *me*. Most boyfriends would have been delighted. But Tommy wasn't having any of it and told my agent that I would not be available to audition. Who knows, maybe I would have got the part, maybe I would have got a different part. Point is, I'll never know. The role went to Sharon Stone, who won a Golden Globe Award and an Oscar nomination for her performance. As I watched my career disintegrate before my eyes, it became harder for me to bury my resentment. I stopped being the fun, sassy Bobbie Brown who Tommy had fallen in love with. I became a bitchy, anorexic tweaker, obsessed with cleaning, who certainly didn't feel like lying around naked with Tommy anymore.

Improbable as this sounds, I did way more drugs than Tommy Lee. At least, during the time we were together. Tommy had already gone through his period of insane drug use with Mötley during the '80s, and by 1994, his lifestyle was relatively tame in comparison. He would do coke socially, maybe one weekend out of a month. At around 7:30 P.M. every night he would make a cocktail and smoke some pot. That was about as wild as he got.

Sometimes we would go down the street to a restaurant that Tommy adored, just to get a shot of this cognac that Tommy loved. It was six hundred dollars a shot, and tasted like soft, very expensive flames licking your throat. Tommy and I always knew how to have fun, even as the cracks began to appear in our relationship.

We went to Japan with Mötley. Things were up-and-down between Tommy and me, as we veered from lovey-dovey to antagonistic from one moment to the next. "I want a tattoo," announced Tommy. "A real yakuza tattoo." Tommy had gotten it into his head that he wanted the Japanese mafia to give him some ink, and our promoter in Japan, a mysterious Japanese gentleman called Mr. Udo, had grudgingly agreed he would help.

We were picked up by one of Mr. Udo's drivers, who drove us through the backstreets of Tokyo in a van with blacked-out windows. We reached a driveway, and a garage door went up, behind which lay a serene compound, a secret yakuza world tucked away from the hustle and bustle on the other side. We entered a building through the back door and went up some stairs to a small studio where the artist was waiting, sitting cross-legged on the floor. He told Tommy to lie on the floor while he drew a traditional *wabori* design; then he inked it on Tommy's skin using not an electric needle, but a needle attached to a long bamboo handle. Tommy was gritting his teeth through the pain, while I checked his face for blackheads. The artist explained to us, through an interpreter, how some yakuza get pearls sewn into their dicks, a sort of "ribbed for pleasure" effect for their women. Tommy laughed and said he was considering getting some, but I rolled my eyes. *Waste of good pearls,* I thought, squeezing a big blackhead on Tommy's chin.

Afterward, we were invited to dinner with Mr. Udo. During the meal I said I was full, which caused the Japanese at the table to erupt in suppressed giggles. "To say you're full in Japanese means you are pregnant," whispered our interpreter.

"Oh, no, not full," I said loudly, pointing to my belly and shaking my head. I plunged my chopsticks into my bowl of rice, leaving them pointing straight up in the air, which prompted more hushed laughter at the table.

"Don't do that, signifies bad omen," said our interpreter. I had grown up on voodoo, gris-gris, and swamp magic, but never before had I met such a superstitious people. Me being me, I took my chopsticks and put them in my ears. "Well, how about this? Bad luck too?"

"Please stop," said the interpreter.

"What about this?" I said, sticking a chopstick up my nose. Mr. Udo smiled politely, and changed the subject.

That night, Tommy and I got in a huge fight in the hotel room. Who knows why? All I knew was that the squabbles were getting meaner and more regular. It didn't help that I was high nearly all the time. I had smuggled meth to Japan in a little matchbox in the pocket of a pair of jeans deep inside my suitcase. Tommy still didn't have a clue that I was using. Poor guy, he just wanted to have fun and enjoy the trip, and kept asking me to go with him to this press event and that party— but I didn't give a shit. All I wanted to do was sit and pick my face in the bathroom mirror. "Fine, Bobbie, stay home and be a weirdo," said Tommy, confused.

DOWNTURN

One weekend, not long after we had returned home to Malibu from Japan, some unexpected visitors showed up—Heather Locklear's sister and her husband. Uninvited and unexpected.

"We just wanted to lie down on the beach, so we thought we'd visit you guys!" It was the weirdest thing ever, but I played it cool. "Sure, come on in." Tommy was also caught off guard, but we were gracious hosts and hung out with them the whole day.

"Tommy, do you think Heather's trying to check up on you or something?" I asked him afterward. He said he was as weirded out as I was about it. Maybe I was paranoid, but I was nobody's fool. It definitely felt to me like her sister had been sent in as a spy. Then, one afternoon, Heather Locklear herself called.

"Oh, hey, girl, what's happening?" said Tommy. *This is too much,* I thought. I couldn't believe how casual he was being with his ex, like it was no biggie that she was calling, even though they hadn't talked in over a year. She asked him something mundane, what their dentist's phone number was or something. Something she could easily have figured out on her own. By now, I was fully spooked. I confronted Tommy.

"What the fuck is going on? Have you guys been seeing each other?"

"Bobbie, you and I spend every waking moment together—how is that even possible?"

"I don't fucking believe you. You're all the same. *Liars!* Once a cheater, always a cheater. Joan Rivers was right."

Tommy was so irritated with me by this point, he got on a plane to Vegas by himself, where he met up with buddies and partied it up for a weekend. That was his payback, his big "fuck you." It was the first time in our relationship that he had gone on vacation without me, aside from touring. I was so mad I packed a bag, and Taylar and I went to stay at Sharise's. When he got back to Malibu, Tommy called and begged me to come home, and after a few days, I did. I thought we had moved on, but a couple of weeks later, the phone rang in the dead of night. A breathy-sounding girl on the line.

"Heyyyy . . . can I speak to Tommy?"

"Who is this?" I asked. The line went dead. Remember, we had a phone service. So anyone who was able to call the house must have gotten the okay from Tommy or me to do so. The next day, I asked the phone company to send me a record of all the numbers that had called. Sure enough, the number had a Vegas dial code. I decided to call this girl, whoever she was, and find out what was going on.

"How do you know Tommy?" I demanded. "I'm his fiancée."

"Oh, I'm sorry, honey. Well, me and my friends spent the night with him in his room. We were having a party."

"Did anything happen?"

"Well, maybe some blow jobs."

When Tommy came home, I quite justifiably raised hell. I wasn't counting on Tommy raising it back at me.

"Fuck you, now you think you're the phone police?" Tommy grabbed me by my hair and dragged me across the living room. My daughter was watching as he threw me on the couch and pinned me down. "What are you, a fucking cop?" I remembered watching my father do the same to my mother. "Go on, hit me," I snarled. Tommy let go. Taylar was crying, and I rushed over to her and held her close.

The next night, Tommy told me he was going to Matt Sorum's house for a party, and that he wanted to go alone. His buddy Elijah Blue showed up and they left the house together. *Fuck that,* I thought, getting dressed. *What am I, Cinderella?* I told Taylar's nanny that I would be home in a few hours, and drove to Matt's house. I walked through the party, and saw Tommy talking to some buddies. We made eye contact and then ignored each other for the rest of the night. I left at around 2 A.M. and went to bed. At around 8 A.M. I was woken up by the sound of Tommy getting home. I walked into the living room and there they were, Tommy and his buddy Whitfield Crane, long-haired lead singer of the band Ugly Kid Joe. Whitfield, this goofy, handsome kid who looked like a surfer, was on our sofa dangling his legs over his head.

"If you were ice cream, what flavor would you be?" Whitfield asked me. "I think you'd be tutti-frutti."

"Fucking clown," I muttered, looking at Tommy. "So why exactly did you bring this asshole home?"

Tommy grabbed me by the arm and marched me to the bedroom and started yelling. Athena and her boyfriend James happened to be staying with us in the guest bedroom. Hearing the commotion, Athena came running into our bedroom. By this point Tommy had me by the throat, pinned against the wall.

"You're a fuckin' bitch!"

Taylar was pulling on his ankles.

"Let her go, you athhhhhole!" she said, with her three-year-old lisp. I punched Tommy in the face, and he loosened his grip around my neck. I fell to the carpet, crying. "Oh, shit . . ." whispered Athena, stunned.

I couldn't believe Taylar was having to witness the very same bullshit I had grown up with as a child. When I got with Tommy, I had no idea he would be violent against women. Now, enough was enough. There was no way Taylar was going to grow up seeing what I had. I told Tommy I was moving out.

ENDLESS BREAKUP

I found a three-bedroom condo in Studio City and moved myself in. Because I had not worked in a year, I had to sell all my jewelry so I could pay my first month's rent and buy Christmas presents for Taylar. I sold my wedding ring, the platinum bracelet Jani had given me, and Tommy's engagement ring. He had asked for it back as I was leaving. "Are you serious? Fuck you, cheese ball!" I screamed, slamming the door behind me.

A few days after Christmas, on December 28, I went back to Tommy's. He had been calling me nonstop, begging me to come home. "No way," I said. "Well, I'm not going to let you in to get your stuff," he said, turning nasty again. "Come on, Tommy, I need my things!"

"I'm not even going to open the door, not until you give me the ring back."

"I don't have the ring, I told you I had to sell it to get my apartment!"

He hung up. I went to see my friend Lene Hefner, a former

Los Angeles Raiders cheerleader turned porn star, and asked if she would come with me to Tommy's to get my stuff. "It's going to be ugly," she said, sounding nervous. "Maybe we should stop at the police station and have them escort us?" We stopped at the cop station that was on the same street as our home, and a nice officer said he would come with us, for protection. The cop rang the doorbell.

"Mr. Lee, I am here with Bobbie Brown—can you open the door, please?"

Tommy opened the door.

"I am here to supervise Miss Brown getting her belongings," said the cop.

"That's not fucking legal. You can't just come here and demand things from me."

"Mr. Lee, her mail still comes here, so legally this is her residence too. She has a right to get her belongings. She felt in fear for her safety and asked me to come along. I am going to ask that you remain in the living room with me while she gathers some things that belong to her and her child."

The cop walked us into the house and stood in the living room. It was beyond awkward. Tommy started following me around the house as I gathered up my things, yelling. "This is my fucking house!" He tried to grab me, and I screamed. The cop came running in. "What happened?"

"He just tried to grab her," said Lene.

"Sir, I am going to ask you not to touch her again."

Tommy, who had lost his grip on reality, went to grab my

arm again. The cop stepped in, put Tommy in cuffs, read him his rights, and took him away in the cop car. I wished things hadn't had to become so dramatic. But that's what Tommy and I were—pure drama. I didn't press charges in the end. As I had tried to explain to Tommy all along, I just wanted my clothes and some plates, knives, and forks for me and Taylar to eat with, dammit!

Most of my furniture from when I lived with Jani was in Tommy's storage unit, so I grabbed the storage unit key that was hanging on the wall, booked a moving van, and went to the unit the following day. When Tommy was released from jail, he must have noticed the key missing, because I opened the door to the unit to find one of Tommy's associates guarding it. As soon as he saw me, he pulled out a gun and pointed it at my head.

"Get the fuck out of here."

He was skinny, with long hair. I knew he was a yes-guy to Tommy, but this was crazy. *What is this*, The Godfather? I thought. I just wanted my couch. I backed away slowly, aghast. No couch was worth getting shot for by Tommy's buddy.

"Have a nice day," he said, slamming the door.

Still, Tommy just wouldn't stop calling. He sent Jay Gordon over to try and hoodwink me into meeting up with him. Jay invited me out for dinner and secretly told Tommy where we were going. When we walked into the restaurant and I saw Tommy there, I couldn't believe it. Tommy came up to me.

"Bobbie—"

"Jay, I can't believe you set me up. I'm leaving!"

I went home and scribbled furiously in my journal. It was the only way I could offload the emotion.

I've tried not to love you, tried to forget you and get on with my life. I recall all the madness, the midnight quarrels, the angry silences and wounding words. Then I remember your smile and the love we once felt. I remember your favorite things in the refrigerator and the love letters you used to fax to me from the road. Your too-tight embraces as we drifted off to sleep. The morning love and our walks on the beach after dinner. Most of all our laughter, so loud and long we forgot what was funny. Last but not least, our shared dreams of our future together. Then my heart aches and impulsively I want to run to your door, share your bed, caress your hair, watch movies, eat root-beer floats, feed the dogs, then laugh some more . . . and share buried hurt. It's then that I miss us most, because quarreling with you has meant more to me than laughing with anyone.

Tommy left me a message saying we needed to talk, and we arranged to meet at a restaurant in Malibu for dinner. He showed up holding twenty or so photos of us together, from happier times. All it did was make me feel defeated. How would we ever be able to be that happy again? "I can't do this, Tommy. I just can't."

Throughout our breakup he had been throwing Pamela's name into the mix, threatening to spend time with her. We both knew she had the hots for him. Even when we were still together, she had a friend of hers call him saying she wanted to hang out. She had a goal, and when Pamela heard we were broken up, it was on. I heard through the grapevine that she and Bret Michaels had broken up. I told Sharise about it. We were in her car and looked at each other like, "Oh no." We both saw what was coming.

On New Year's Eve, I tried to celebrate as best I could—which was hard, as I found myself at the same party as Tommy, there with Pamela Anderson. What a surprise.

"Fuck!" said Sharise, nodding toward them. They were at a table, flirting, drinking, and laughing. "You okay?"

"Sure," I said, playing it cool. Nonetheless, our friend Becky Mullen marched up to their table.

"What you're doing is really fucked-up, Tommy," she said. "Don't be flirting with other people in front of Bobbie."

"Dude, why'd you do that?" I said when she came back. I was embarrassed. I didn't want them thinking I cared. Of course I cared. I was just very good at pretending to be a hard-ass.

Even after that, Tommy continued to call. Sometimes he'd be sweet, sometimes he'd dangle the Pamela threat, trying to make me jealous. But I stood my ground. Shortly before Valentine's Day, Tommy convinced me to let him come over to my new place. Within minutes the situation had degenerated into a huge fight. In the heat of the moment, he took a bottle and threw it at the wall. Red wine splattered across the room, droplets hitting my daughter's face. I looked at my little girl, her skin dripping with Merlot. It was like a scene out of *Carrie*. She started crying, and I flipped out. "Get the fuck out of here! You destroy everything! I don't have a dime and you are kicking holes in the wall and breaking things in the presence of my daughter." As he drove home, Tommy called me, crying. A Mary J. Blige song had come on the radio, and it was killing him listening to the lyrics, he said.

I'm goin' down
Cause you ain't around, baby

"I'm really sad," he said.
"I'm really sad too."
"I'm sorry."
As in love as we were, it was just obvious nothing was going to work itself out with us. There was nothing more to say. I knew that in relationships, once things reach a certain point, they don't get better, they only get worse. That night, I knew we were officially over.

Two days later, Tommy left a message on my answering machine.

"I'm in Cancún with Pamela Anderson. We have sex toys. I'm going to fuck her really hard."

Just the sound of his voice made my stomach churn. I played the message to Sharise.

"Listen to this motherfucker."

We made his message into my voice mail greeting, Sharise and I yelling, "Leave a message after the douchebag," at the end. Tommy was furious. "Come on, Bob, that's not cool, what the fuck? Please get rid of it, Bobbie, I'm really sorry."

Two days after that, the phone rang—it was our mutual friend Bobby, calling long-distance from Mexico. By this point, Tommy and I had been officially broken up exactly four days.

"Bobbie, I'm in Cancún with Tommy and Pamela, and they're getting married. Tommy wanted me to call and let you know."

"Right. Whatever, dude, they deserve each other, they're both fucking assholes," I said. "Hold on—you *are* kidding, right?"

Bobby described the chain of events to me. Pamela had flown out to Cancún on a photo shoot, right around the time Tommy and I were breaking up. The day he smashed the wine bottle in my house, Tommy called Pamela and told her he was getting on a plane. Tommy landed, they had dinner, and Tommy proposed. Three days later, on February 18, they went to a hospital at two in the morning to get their blood tests done. And then, all of day four of their relationship, they were tying the knot. *What kind of joke did Tommy think he was playing on me now?*

All day long, Bobby called me with the play-by-play breakdown of the day's surreal events.

"They're saying they're really in love."

"No shit!" I screamed.

"They just got married, Bobbie, on the beach."

"They really got married? You weren't fucking with me?"

"They are married, Bobbie."

In a furious daze, I called every journalist I knew and told them to come to my apartment. Within twenty minutes *People* magazine, *Us Weekly*, *Star*, and a camera crew from *American Journal* had shown up. They sat in front of me, expectant and slightly confused. I tried to steady my nerves. I didn't want to cry in front of them. "I would like to inform the press that my fiancé, Tommy Lee, married Pamela Anderson on the beach in Cancún this afternoon. Perhaps you'd like to visit them to pass on my congratulations." I told them the name of their hotel and their room number.

"Don't you want any money for this, Bobbie?" one of the journalists asked, and I said no. This wasn't about money. This was about my heart, which had just been broken into a million pieces. *American Journal* wanted to interview me on camera. I shouldn't have agreed, but I did. When the interview played on TV afterward, I was horrified. I was super skinny, crying, a mess. I never meant for the world to see me like that. I felt humiliated. But the humiliation had just begun.

I watched the tragicomedy unfold on TV, in the tabloids, around the world. They called it a "Madcap Marriage." I saw the photos of Pamela, barefoot and in a white bikini on the beach with Tommy, and eight guests, many of them my friends, lying on sun loungers holding cocktails in plastic cups while a Mexican guy in a white suit read their vows. Even behind her aviator sunglasses, I could tell Pamela was wasted. Bobby said they were all on ecstasy. Then they kissed, and Tommy tossed Pamela into the Caribbean. Sadly, she didn't drown. Pamela's own mother found out about the wedding by reading about it in *People* magazine. It was the first she had heard of Tommy Lee, and she called the whole thing "heartbreaking and shocking." I knew exactly how she felt.

Chapter Nine

DOUCHE PARADE

Biker coffee, glass, crank, whatever you want to call it—it's a dirty chemistry that gives rise to speed. They make it in laboratories far, far away from Tinseltown; in trailers in Desert Hot Springs, or manufacturing plants in Guadalajara. Sudafed pills, Drano, lighter fluid, rubbing alcohol, paint thinner, red phosphorus from matchbooks, iodine, and battery acid create an inhumane and potent brew that leaves the user wide-eyed and sweaty, fingers tapping on tables, thoughts rushing with unhinged intensity. Life becomes the thing that happens in between key bumps in bathrooms, or breaking up lines with maxed-out cards. Then you grind your teeth on the dance floor as the flashing lights tell you things in languages only you can understand. Outside, the trees seem alive, clouds flicker like strobes, and the wind seems to quote lines from movies. The sun is always a little too bright. I was running while standing still, floating when I walked. The car rides, talking talking talking, the conversations that meant so much and would count for nothing the second I walked into my upper-middle-class condo in the Valley, remembering that my lover was with someone else. I wanted to scratch my nails down my cheeks until they bled.

There was a knock at the door. I opened it, hoping it might be Tommy, saying this had all been a big prank, one of his jokes. But it was my mother, looking stern. "Tommy wrote me a letter, Bobbie, saying you are a drug addict. I've come to get Taylar because I don't want my granddaughter around that nonsense." I slammed the door in her face. "Fuck you! We're fine!" I didn't want my mom around, judging me, seeing what a failure I really was. But she kept knocking and knocking, until I let her back in. She was horrified at how skinny I was—around ninety pounds at the time. She told me how she had gotten Tommy's letter the day before he married Pamela. "I wrote him back saying 'fuck you,'" said my mom, who, as I mentioned before, almost never curses. "And I told him, 'If anything bad happens to my daughter because of all this, I am going to hold you *personally* responsible.'" My mother took Taylar back to Louisiana with her. From that point, Taylar's childhood would be a merry-go-round, with her going back and forth between L.A. and my mom's, depending on how messed up I was over some guy, or the drugs. That's the only true regret I have in my life: that thanks to drugs, "love," and my own dysfunction, I was so rarely able to be the mother I wanted to be.

As my mom left, she told me to pull myself together. "Get over it, Bobbie. He wasn't good for you." I wished getting over Tommy could have been that simple. I was on antidepressants but none of them worked. All I wanted to do was stay in bed in the fetal position and cry. The only thing that would get me moving was speed. At least when I was high, I had the energy to try to forge ahead with my day, even though the guy I was in love with had just gotten married and it was all over the news.

Every time I left my apartment, there they were, on the newsstands. They were going out of their way to court every possible photo opportunity, and Pamela was all about the publicity. It was sickening. I felt like an unwilling observer, trapped in their romance, forced to watch them kiss every day, all day long. People would come up to me saying, "Hey, it's really sad about Tommy," which made me feel even worse. I didn't want anyone feeling sorry for me.

"Bobbie? Bobbie, are you okay? Let us in!"

It was my friend Annie, knocking on the front door. I opened the door, my face smeared with mascara. She was with her boyfriend Doug. They had just come from Tommy and Pamela's wedding reception, where Doug, who I had introduced to Tommy, had been best man.

Naturally, they felt guilty about having to split their loyalties. But I wasn't angry, I was just grateful that they were there with me. "Pamela is such a retard," said Annie, giving me a hug. The reception had been a lavish, over-the-top affair, with Tommy dressed in a suit of armor. "A suit of armor? That's weird," I sniffed, pouring more wine.

Pamela had already been doing all she could to wipe me off the face of Hollywood. *Playboy* was already off-limits, thanks to her. Now, *Baywatch*. I had been on a series of auditions, vying for a role in the show, auditions that had started as Tommy and I were breaking up. Getting that part would have been a lifeline, a chance to start my career over. The producers could not decide between me and Gena Lee Nolin. Unsurprisingly, Pamela stepped in at the eleventh hour and told them there was no way she would work with me. It was understandable, but it wasn't fair. The role went to Gena.

At the wedding reception, Doug and Annie had met one of Tommy's friends, a singer by the name of Mark McGrath. Mark was in a band called Shrinky Dinx (after the Shrinky Dinks toy), which would soon change its name to Sugar Ray. Mark had came over with Doug and Annie—I think they were hoping Mark might lift my spirits. Their instincts had been correct.

"Girl, I would eat your pussy for eighteen hours straight, if it helped," he said, moments after being introduced, startling me into laughter. Mark had zero filter. And he was funny. His inappropriate humor was bringing me out of my depressive funk for a minute. I wanted to see him again. "Mark, I have a modeling shoot tomorrow. Will you come with me?" I asked him at the end of the night. I just didn't want to be alone. "Sure," he said, without a thought, and I loved him immediately.

Mark's band Sugar Ray was not known yet, so he wasn't busy, touring all the time like Tommy had been. We started hanging out every day doing silly mundane stuff: grocery shopping, picking up underwear at Sears. Stuff that helped me maintain some illusion of sanity. And of course, when the daytime chores had been taken care of, we partied. Mark and I were out at a club one night when a small brunette girl came up and tapped me on the shoulder. "Hey, I'm Carin, Mark's girlfriend." *What?!* Mark hadn't mentioned anything about having a girlfriend. *Is this a joke?* "I'm sorry," I said. "For the record, there's nothing going on between us. Maybe you need to talk to Mark about this, not me." Mark walked up to us, looking guilty. For a second, I hated him. "You guys have fun working this out. I'm leaving," I said, heading for the door. *Is there any man in this town who isn't a liar?* I thought, hurt. Mark looked at me, then at Carin. Then at me and back at Carin. "I'm sorry, Carin, I'm going with Bobbie," he said, darting after me. (They had not been dating for a long time, though he is married to her today.)

"Why didn't you tell me you had a girlfriend?" I asked Mark in the car. I was too tired to be angry.

"Dunno." He shrugged.

"Why can't you guys just be *honest*?"

"Because we suck?" said Mark, looking sheepish.

"Well, just be careful, I'm kind of vulnerable right now," I said, sniffing. "You're lucky I didn't rip your balls off."

I was trying to get my life back on track, but it was hard. I had to move out of my apartment because I could no longer afford it, and I was desperate for work. When my agency booked me a weeklong job in Miami, I breathed a sigh of relief. I was going to be good this time, no speed for Bobbie. I was a professional, and I was going to get my life together. In some misguided attempt to be responsible, I decided to use up all my drugs in the few weeks before Miami, so at least I would be sober on the job. Bad idea. By the time I got to Miami I was so partied out, I realized I should have just brought the drugs with me just to keep me awake. But I didn't have any left, and I didn't have the money to score. The result? During the first day of shooting, I passed out during several shots, drooling as my eyes rolled into the back of my head. Then, when I went back to the hotel, I stayed up all night, writing poems with metallic Sharpie pens in my notebook, waking up covered in ink, the bedspread ruined because I had forgotten to put the lids back on the pens. A five-year-old would have had better sense. That day, I nodded off throughout the shoot, again. "That girl is on heroin," muttered the photographer. The client called my agency saying I was on drugs. *I wished.* I was just sleep-deprived. On day three, unsurprisingly, they fired me, and I was sent home with a bill for the ruined bedspread. I flew to New Orleans in tears, planning to pick up my daughter and go back to L.A., but my dad met me at the airport and told me I wasn't allowed to go to my mom's and get Taylar until I had gotten myself straight. I flipped out.

"I want to be with my daughter!" I yelled, calling my mom from my dad's house phone.

"No," said my mom on the end of the line. "Not until you are sober. You're staying at your dad's until you get yourself together, Bobbie."

My dad put me to bed, and I slept for five days straight. When I woke up, I was ravenous. "That's some, ahem, flu you had there, girl," said my dad, watching me pour my third bowl of Lucky Charms. I glared at him. Of course, he was aware of my problems, but he knew better than to confront me about my addiction at this point. I stayed with my poppa for two weeks, watching *Oprah*, eating carbs, and crying, until I finally regained my senses, my sobriety, and a couple of pounds. "You know, this is the most time we've spent together since your momma kicked me out," said my dad as he hugged me good-bye, a tear in his eye. "Just remember you're not alone in this, Bobbie. You're not alone." I don't know why I found it so hard to believe him.

NIGHT MOVES

I was at Grand Ville. I needed something. *Someone.* I looked around. *Let's see . . . model, wannabe, model, actor, model, rocker, drug dealer, model.* What a douche parade. I hadn't been with anyone since Tommy Lee, but now, finally, Bobbie Brown was open for business.

"I gotta say, I feel sorry for the first guy who sleeps with you," said Sharise.

"Why?"

"Well, after Tommy, he's going to have to nail his dick to a two-by-four just to keep it from falling out."

"Ha-ha, very funny," I said, noticing a cute guy in the corner. "Wait, who's *that?*"

Standing with the actor/club promoter BoJesse Christopher was a beautiful man with dark hair and icy blue eyes that seemed to glow. BoJesse introduced us: His name was Jason, and he was a model. I made it clear that I was available, and a few hours later, Jason was massaging my back on my bed. As his fingers kneaded my shoulders, I drifted into a deep sleep. When I woke up, he was kissing me, grinding on top of me, and making moaning sounds.

"Arghgh!"

Why is he making that noise? I wondered. He groaned even louder.

"Orghgh!"

Then he rolled over and lit up a cigarette. "That was so amazing, baby." It took me a second to figure it out. I had not even realized that I was being fucked. I ran into the bathroom, and checked myself. Was it a black hole, incapable of sensation? *Jesus, maybe Sharise was right! Maybe Tommy had stretched me beyond the point of no return!* I was so horrified, I told Jason to get out. I couldn't believe that this was how my first time after Tommy had gone down. I didn't feel victorious—I felt cheated. Of course, poor Jason was completely confused by my sudden change of attitude.

"No, we're not going to snuggle, Jason. You got what you wanted, now beat it!" I had never been this mean to a lover before, in my life.

"Are you joking, Bobbie?" Jason said, looking hurt.

"Do I *look* like I'm joking? You better be out of here by the time I count to five." Jason called me all the next day, and when I finally picked up, I was businesslike. "State your purpose," I said. Being a bitch felt empowering.

Somehow, Jason and I remained friends and years later, over lunch, he decided to reminisce about our one night of "passion."

"You know . . . when you and I had sex, it was pretty wild and crazy," he said, with a half smile.

I said, "Jason, you're kidding, right? Bless your heart, you need to get out more."

I wasn't trying to be a dick. I swear.

Next!

Leonardo DiCaprio, some model dude, the actor Billy Wirth, some singer, Kevin Costner, some hip-hop dancer—whether it was kisses or blow jobs or promises or druggy nights or shitty sex, I could barely keep track of all the men in my field of vision. They all looked the same to me now. Even the ones I had known for years. Thankfully, after my numbed-out experience with Jason, I had begun to actually feel the sex I was having. But I spent a blurry, shut-down year of my life inviting men into my world and then casting them aside the following morning, or not long after, usually in the cruelest manner possible. Fucking the douche parade as a means of revenge was not my lowest point; rather, it became just one in a series of poorly thought-out coping strategies. I just couldn't think up any other way to shut out my anger. So I fucked the pain away instead.

In 1996, less than a year after Tommy wed Pamela, their sex tape came out, rubbing salt into my still-raw wounds. I couldn't go anywhere without some asshole putting it on the VHS. I'd be at party, go to the bathroom, and then come out to the sound of Pamela squealing.

"I love you, Tommy!"

Ugh, not again.

They were on a yacht. She was grasping for his dick with her long, manicured nails. It made me want to hurl.

"Whip it out. Whip it *out!*"

Oh, there was the house Tommy and I were supposed to move into.

"This is our house," said Pamela. "When are you going to get me preggos?"

Now she's giving him head in the car. Road dome. Classy.

I couldn't believe Tommy would have filmed all this. He never once expressed any interest in filming our sex life. I assumed it must have been Pamela's idea. She had made a sex tape with Bret Michaels too, and I had seen the footage of her sucking him off, naked on the bed, to the sound of some atrocious heavy metal. That video was just funny. This, on the other hand, was painful.

"Fuck, I'm so fucking horny," says Tommy. Then they pull over and have sex on the side of the road. "I love you, I love you, I love you," Tommy says into the camera, mouthing the words. "He has a huge fucking wenis. And big balls," says Pamela, before the film cuts to Tommy's huge fucking wenis entering her perfectly-shaved pussy. *Wonderful.*

Around the same time, in 1996, Jani remarried. Even though I had never seriously contemplated reuniting with him, his moving on somehow made me feel even more alone. His second wife was Rowanne Brewer, a former Miss Maryland, who gave birth to their daughter, Madison, the following year. I knew Rowanne from the modeling circuit, and we had been friends when I was married to Jani. We shot a Budweiser commercial together, and I remember thinking she was attractive and friendly. When I was with Tommy, I heard that she was hitting on him, which upset me. Then, next thing you know, she marries Jani. *I guess we have similar taste in men,* I thought. Jani had been drinking since our divorce, and, from what I heard, was drunk for the majority of his marriage with Rowanne. Even at a distance, Jani's dysfunction depressed me. He was still the father of my child, after all.

Pamela filed for divorce from Tommy in November 1996. *Figures,* I thought, remembering how quickly Tommy had devolved from handsome Prince Charming into mini dictator when we were together. Days after news of the divorce broke, Tommy called me. My hand trembled as I gripped the phone and heard what he had to say. I had missed him so much. He said wanted to make amends. Would I be willing to see him? I hadn't talked to Tommy since our breakup, and there had been no closure whatsoever. Maybe Pamela filing for divorce had been some kind of wake-up call. Maybe this would help me heal. Maybe we would get back together. Of course, that was what I was hoping for. I was still desperately in love with him.

I left a note for my brother, who was staying with me, on the coffee table. "I'm not going to be home tonight, I'll be at Tommy's—explain later."

I arrived at Tommy's house in Malibu—the house Tommy

and I were supposed to move into. Tommy seemed upbeat. It was weird. It had taken all the emotional strength I had to even be there, and even more just to look him in the eye. I was still so heartbroken. But he was behaving like nothing had ever happened. "Let's go upstairs!" he said. "I want to show you the beanbag room." *The beanbag room. Okay.*

The beanbag room had a floor that was entirely soft and squishy. They used it as their movie room, I guess. I stepped in and started laughing, surprised by the odd sensation. Out of the blue, Tommy lunged at my feet and tackled me to the soft floor.

"Look at that ass!" he said, flipping me over. Then he put his face in between my ass cheeks and made motorboat noises, before collapsing in giggles.

"What the fuck!" I screamed. I fought back the tears.

"What's wrong, dude?" said Tommy, confused. The playful energy in the room vanished as I unloaded my hurt.

"Last time I saw you we were engaged; then you dumped my ass and married Pamela! Now you're putting your face in my ass? What the *fuck*! Why do you have to be such a *child*!"

Tommy told me not to cry and tickled me. I couldn't help but break into laughter in between tears. Tommy's casual demeanor was luring me into a false sense of security. He had always been so good at that, at joking away the pain. Tommy cuddled me and said he wanted me to stay the night. I looked around the room—the decor was feminine, there were knickknacks I knew didn't belong to him. I could feel Pamela in the room with us. It felt creepy.

"I don't think so, Tommy." But Tommy Lee gets what Tommy Lee wants. Almost.

I ended up staying. We didn't sleep together, we didn't even kiss. But we laughed all night long, until at some point in the wee hours, he fell asleep. I was high, of course, and just lay there, mind racing, heart pounding. When dawn broke, I wrote him a note, left it on the pillow, and tiptoed out. "Had a good time, got to go, bye."

After that he came over to my place one day; another night we went to a party. Still, nothing sexual happened, but he was calling me every day. I started to wonder . . . could I do this again with Tommy? Was there a chance for us? One day he called and said he had to go out of town to do something with Snoop Dogg for a few days. I didn't hear from him again. I read that he had gotten back with Pam. Within two weeks of filing for divorce, she had called it off, and all was forgiven. As I struggled to process the hurt and anger of being rejected a second time, I thanked God I hadn't allowed anything to happen between Tommy and me. Because that would have fucking annihilated me.

(It wouldn't be too long before Pamela would file for divorce a second time. In early '98, Tommy was led from their house in Malibu in handcuffs after Pamela accused him of attacking her as she held their two-month-old second son, Dylan. Tommy went to jail for four months for spousal battery. Again, I wasn't surprised.) I cried myself to sleep for a few nights at my town house in the Valley, cursing myself for letting Tommy back in, even for just a second. And then I got back to what I knew best—the club scene and my new best friend, crystal meth.

At first I liked crystal because it made me skinny. Then I liked crystal because it had become part of my daily routine. *Wake up, brush teeth, feed dog, do bump.* One hit would last me about eight hours, and it wasn't even expensive. Unlike coke, this seemed like a healthy habit to have. *This doesn't feel like a problem at all,* I told myself, admiring my figure in the mirror, enjoying the energetic high I felt every day.

I had been sober, off of coke for five years when someone offered me a line and I figured it couldn't hurt. Then I remembered why cocaine didn't agree with me. The comedowns, for me, were suicidally awful. I felt depressed and guilty. I could never sleep properly because all I wanted was more coke. I would need another line, need another line, need another line. Coke would make me want to stay locked in with the lights low, talking about stupid shit that didn't mean dick for hours, saying creepy shit and doing creepy shit. I didn't want to go out into the daylight and accomplish my goals, hell no. With crystal, things were different. When the high fades, you just pass out cold because you are so tired from being up for three, four, five days straight. On speed, I was more than happy to leave the house and run errands, which I enjoyed so much more than the whole dungeon vibe of cocaine nights. But, as energetic as the speed made me, there was a downside. Speed brain.

Speed would render me slightly autistic, in the sense that it would make me tunnel-vision on the most mundane of things. I would quite happily spend an hour and a half sitting down and cutting a piece of paper. Meth-fueled crafting became a big part of my life. My favorite reward after finishing a modeling job would be to go Michaels, buy a bunch of crafting supplies—glitter, felt, neon paints, googly eyes, yarn—then come home and go crazy with the glue gun. For, like, *days*. "Watch out, I will glue your ass to the wall," I'd tell my friends when they came over. I was making journals and writing poetry in gold glitter ink and doing whatever felt like fun. I became a pretty badass crafter when I was on speed. If only Etsy had existed back then, I might have made a fortune.

I would go through phases where I stopped using for a while. That's when I would go to the gym, join spin classes, book this modeling job and that modeling job. But as soon as there was a lull, I would get bored and start partying again. Or if I started to gain weight, I would immediately freak out and start using. I'll say this, when you book a swimwear job and have to lose fifteen pounds within a week, speed delivers. It amps up your metabolism so much, the weight slides off like butter from a hot potato. For someone like me, who had always been body conscious, crystal meth was the cure-all panacea I had been waiting for all my life. I didn't care about the speed brain. Not even when things started getting really trippy.

Before the government started regulating the over-the-counter sale of pseudoephedrine (a key ingredient in crystal), speed was insanely strong. On one hit, I could be up for four days before feeling sleepy. Depriving your body of sleep for such extended periods, you start hearing and seeing shit that quite simply is not there. You enter a new realm of existence, populated by shadows, spirits, and demons that you catch glimpses of in the corner of your eye. Sometimes, my own body would play tricks on me. I would be standing there, holding a drink, and suddenly, I would pour it over my own head. Strange things were afoot.

Since then, I've read some spiritual, New Age–type of books about what can happen to your soul when you are an addict. They say that addiction can make a person vulnerable to malevolent energies that may start using your body as a conduit. Who knows the truth, but things got freaky. At the height of my addiction, I would walk into a party, then feel something push me so hard I would go flying and land on my face in the middle of the floor. To the people around me, it just seemed like maybe I was epileptic, or drunk, or both. But to me it was like something otherworldly was playing tricks on me. Poor Kevin Costner— how was he to know that his speed-freak date was potentially being toyed with by malicious entities who were using her body as a portal? As I lay facedown on Kevin's carpet, trying to own it by cheerfully yelling, "Face-plant!" I couldn't help but wonder if my body even belonged to me anymore.

HOOLIGAN'S HOLIDAY

Danny Boy, lead singer of House of Pain, had turned into something of a personal bodyguard for me. Between him, Sharise, Annie, and my flirty new BFF Mark McGrath, I never felt alone. Thank God for friends. It was the first time since I had arrived in Los Angeles that I had been single, and their support pretty much saved me.

Danny Boy would stay over at my condo in Studio City for days on end and laugh at whoever I would bring back. One night he came downstairs to find some guy sucking my fingers while I was half-asleep on the couch. "Hey, dude, go get a fucking meal if you're hungry," said Danny Boy, scaring the shit out of the guy and waking me up.

"What's happening?" I said, drowsy.

"Homeboy here was eating your arm. Hey, I can take him to Burger King if you like."

Another time, I woke up in my bed with some guy humping my leg. I kicked him out of my bed with the full force of both my legs, and he landed with a yelp—remember, my bed was pretty much on stilts. "Danny Boy! Some fool's rubbing up on my leg!" Danny Boy came running in, looking mean. "Hey, Superhump. Time to go."

If we were out and a guy started hitting on me, Danny Boy would get in his face.

"You okay, Bob?"

"Yeah, I'm fine, babe, fuck off!"

"Okay, cool, I didn't realize you were shopping."

Danny was like the big brother I never had. Yes, he had tried to hit on me, right at the beginning of our friendship. But we nipped that in the bud pretty fast.

"I think I could love you," he said, dreamy lust in his eyes.

"What?"

"I know you were with Tommy, but I don't need you to pinch my nipples and pour wax over me. I'm not freaky like that."

"Stop!"

"Really, you're not trying to hook up?" He was surprised that I could want to spend this much time with him and not want to have sex. But "friend-zoning"—having pseudo boyfriends with whom I would never have sex—was something of a specialty for me.

When I told Danny I was going on a date with John Corabi, Tommy's bandmate in Mötley Crüe, he just shook his head and laughed. "You're on a hooligan's holiday, girl," he said. I wasn't sure what he meant, and then the penny dropped—it was the title of a Mötley song. John picked me up in his car—I can't remember what kind.

"Let's go to my place," he said, and I agreed, feeling giddy about doing this with one of Tommy's bandmates. *The ultimate revenge.* I went to John's house and stayed the night, doing nothing but making out like teenagers. In the end though, I just could not bone down with that dude. Not only was it weird that I was doing this with one of Tommy's bandmates, it was weird that he was making out with *me*. I remembered how in the rock scene, guys always seemed to have so little loyalty to one another—in that world, it's each dick for himself. I promised myself I would never *ever* make out with any member of Mötley Crüe, ever again.

Next!

Mark McGrath, after months of flirting, joking, druggy nights, and innuendo, was about to get his shot.

"Okay, Mark, you're up."

I figured we might as well just get it over with. I was already acting all girlfriendy with him, taking acne cream over to his place when he complained of having breakouts and buying him presents.

"We're going to do this."

"Really? You're serious?"

"Yep, now. Get naked and get in bed."

He was tripping over his pants.

"I feel like I'm on *The Love Boat*."

Just as it had with Tommy, months of friendship and "platonic" hanging out had created quite the buildup. Whether the sex was "good" or "bad" wasn't an issue. It just felt exciting to be intimate with someone who I cared about as a friend, and whose company I enjoyed so much. Which is why it annoyed me when he started acting all insecure.

"You can't even feel this, can you?" He wasn't especially big, but I didn't care.

"Stop saying that!"

"Bobbie, is my dick too small?"

"Shut *up!*"

Of course, the more we slept together, the closer we became. Even though it was supposed to be a casual "friends with benefits" type of thing. Soon I became "the problem" in his relationship with Carin. For my part, I was distressed about breaking my rule of sleeping with men who had girlfriends. But Mark and Carin were so on and off, it was hard to keep track of what was going on. Mark and I seemed to spend more time together than they did. It was strange, and none of our friends really understood what was happening between us. I don't think we did either. All I wanted from Mark was him to continue to make me laugh. As long as the fun and the partying lasted, I wouldn't have to deal with my problems.

Next!

Poor Bryce. He was a model guy, truly convinced that he was the hottest shit in town. Great-looking, tall and muscular, he had all the girls in love with him, and he knew it. I decided that he would be a perfect candidate for me to flip the script on. I was hanging out with Bobby Hewitt, the drummer of Orgy, and his new girlfriend Shannon, who would become his wife. Bryce and I went back to their house after a night on the dance floor.

Maybe I'll fuck him and send him home in a cab, I thought. Guys *hated* it when I did that. When Bryce went to the bathroom, I told Bobby and Shannon I was going to take Bryce outside and screw him on their trampoline. They were amused by this and found themselves a good vantage point from which to spy on us.

I took Bryce into their backyard and pulled him onto the trampoline. The thought of him trying to bounce on top of me was making me giggle. We started kissing and getting into it. Then he murmured, "Hey, do you have any spit?"

"Excuse me?"

Maybe Bryce had cottonmouth from the drugs we had been doing. Maybe he was hoping for some spit to grease up his weiner. But what was I supposed to do, hock a loogie on his junk?

"No, I do not have any extra spit on me. Don't ever in the future say that to anybody ever again. That is seriously the biggest turnoff of all time."

I hopped off the trampoline and grabbed my bag. I was out of there. Over it.

"Wait, don't you want me to come home with you?" he said.

"I don't know. And before you ask, no, I don't have any spit in the fridge."

He followed me home and repeatedly attempted to seal the deal, even though by this point I was fully over it. Bryce the Adonis could not wrap his head around the fact that a woman was turning him down. It simply did not compute.

"Girl, you know you want this," he said, grabbing my hand again, pulling it toward his crotch. I snatched it away, exasperated.

"Bryce, look at me. I don't want 'this.' And I don't want to give you spit. Now here's some money for a cab. I'm going to the store, and I would love it if you could not be here by the time I get back."

Thankfully, Bryce and his spittle-deficient mouth had bailed by the time I returned.

For months after that, his friends would come up to me. "What did you do to Bryce? You totally messed with his head!" One day he messaged me. *Now I understand what love means, and that is thanks to you.* I rolled my eyes and laughed.

Next!

I met this cute kid called Stevie Sculthorpe, a singer and model in a band called Take 5. He looked young. Really young. Like, nearly as young as Leo. But he told me he was twenty-six, so I took him at his word. We kissed a couple of times, and my girlfriend Lisa started hanging out with one of the other kids in his band, so she and I went together to one of their showcases, where I introduced myself to Stevie's mom. "Your son is so talented, Mrs. Sculthorpe!" I said, "and he really knows how to dance." She just scowled and walked away. I could not believe how cold and mean she was. *Poor Stevie,* I thought.

I stood side-stage and watched the guys do their solo performances, after which they each introduced themselves to the audience.

"Hi, my name's Stevie Sculthorpe, I'm seventeen, from Miami, Florida."

Wait. *Seventeen?* I screamed and ran out of there. He was

still in high school! *No wonder his mom hated me so much!* I had unwittingly been playing Mrs. Robinson. A few nights later I ran into Tilky Jones, one of Steve's bandmates, and he said Steve's mom had wanted to call the police on me. I didn't blame her! Her teenage son was hanging out with Tommy Lee's ex-fiancée? What a nightmare. Embarrassed as I was, I ended up making out with Tilky too (he was a ripe old nineteen) and then ignored both their calls. Talk about jailbait.

Next!

Shane West was a handsome actor who, like me, is from Louisiana. I ran into him at a Wild West–themed bar/restaurant on the Strip called Saddle Ranch.

"Bobbie Brown?"

"Yes?"

"I'm a Southern kid too. How are you?"

He flashed me a smile and his familiar accent immediately put me at ease. *Thank God,* I thought, *someone with manners.* Something happens to people when they live in Hollywood for too long—the ambition, the pressure to be more than what you are, it can make people pushy and selfish. You even see it on the freeway—L.A. drivers are notorious for cutting you off, for yelling, and for not letting you pass. It's a hyper-competitive town on all levels, and often people won't make the time to talk to you if you don't fit into their "plan" in some way—that's just the Hollywood way. In a town like that, it can be hard to make real friends.

When we started sleeping together, I realized that as much

as I was digging his vibe, there might be a little compatibility issue. Shane was the kind of guy who would wake up and want to make out before brushing his teeth, which grossed me out because he drank a lot and his morning breath was brutal. One night he played a show with his band and invited me to come and watch. *Oh, I wish you hadn't done that,* I thought, standing side-stage. The music really wasn't to my taste. Afterward we went back to his house and he wanted to fool around.

"Don't you want to shower first?" I said, imagining his sweaty balls. "You've just been onstage for two hours."

"No, baby, who cares." *Ew,* I thought.

We had been seeing each other several nights a week, so I kind of assumed that we were exclusive. I stopped seeing other guys and stopped returning their calls. It was nice to feel like there might be something special happening between Shane and me. Then one night I was chatting with a girl out at a club, telling her how I was dating Shane, when she informed me that Shane might not be as devoted as he seemed.

"Bobbie, I was at his place just the other night with a video recorder, taping him fucking this other girl. I'm sorry."

I was furious. I went to his place and threw trash all over his car.

"You're a scumbag!" I screamed at him.

"But, Bobbie, we're not exclusive!" he protested.

"Then why did you have to go *acting* all exclusive? Or is that just what actors do? Listen, I'm not going to be loyal to someone who is fucking other people. I don't like to share dick, you know what I mean?"

Next!

I brought home the MTV VJ Simon Rex one night. He was a good-looking kid who would later became known for dating Paris Hilton. Simon had also done a sex tape, a solo one, called *Young, Hard & Solo III* (am I the only person on earth who hasn't done a sex tape?). I met Simon through Bryce, who had gotten over the humiliation of being dissed by me, and now we were all friends. Simon had a sweet, private-school kind of charm to him, and we started hooking up after the clubs. Three weeks into it, he called me, saying he needed to talk.

"Bobbie, I have to be honest—my ex came back around and she wants to try and work things out. I'm going to give it a shot, so you know, we have to go back to being just friends."

I had mad respect for him for being up-front. Finally, a man who wasn't afraid to just tell the truth.

"Simon, I'm glad you called me, and I think it is admirable that you guys are going to try and work things out. Thanks for being honest with me. You don't know how much that means."

Not long after, I was at a commercial casting, when this cute brunette actress girl sat next to me.

"Hey, are you Bobbie Brown?"

"Yes, that's me," I said, looking up from my *Us Weekly*.

"I hear you know Simon . . . Simon Rex?"

"Yes, he's sweet."

"You guys hooking up?" I was a little taken aback at being asked about my personal life by a stranger. But I had nothing to hide.

"We were. It was nothing serious, though, you know. We're just friends now."

I came home later that night to a hysterical voice mail from Simon.

"I can't believe you told my girlfriend about us!"

Huh? I was confused.

I called him, and he was freaking out.

"You're a bitch, Bobbie Brown!"

I had admired Simon for his honesty, until learning he hadn't extended the gesture to his girlfriend.

"Listen, I had no idea she was your girlfriend. It was entrapment, dude!"

But he continued to call me names. *That's it,* I thought, hanging up. *I'm fucking done with this shit!*

That night, while I waited for the club kids to come pick me up, I cried while scribbling furiously in my journal:

Tonight we go out. To seem somehow like a shining star to those who could care less, and to some who should care more. On the exterior, shiny and new for all to view. But they don't see the real me, for today I'm empty and walking in the shadow of someone I used to be. What false feeling will I dress up as tonight? Will my soul creep out or will I be able to just be alive, at least pull off breathing? Who even cares? I pretend

they do. And regardless I'll shine, be blind and strut around
with my ears closed. I wear a mask, as you do too. To hide
what none has time to comprehend. A mask to hide how little
I care for anything but to find real friends and true lovers.

At Grand Ville, Sharise nudged me hard. "Look, it's that ass-hole Simon Rex!" He was hanging out by the bar, laughing and joking, looking nothing like a guy who had just lost the love of his life, and who had yelled at me on the phone just hours earlier. I asked Sharise if she wouldn't mind going up to Simon and giving him a piece of her mind, on my behalf. "My pleasure," she said, marching in his direction. I smiled as I watched Sharise tear Simon a brand-new asshole. I couldn't hear what she was saying, but when she pointed over in my direction, my eyes met with his. I slowly raised up my middle finger, stuck the finger in my mouth and licked it slowly up and down before flipping him off. Sharise, I could see, was bent double, laughing.

Chapter Ten
IF YOU WANT MY BODY

The year or so following my breakup with Tommy Lee in early 1995 had been a haze of catastrophic dates, failed relationships, and inappropriate hookups, punctuated by short-lived attempts to get sober, during which I would usually show up in Baton Rouge, tail between my legs, seeking refuge from Hollywood and the people in it. Inevitably, I would return to L.A., full of good intentions and AA-sanctioned gratitude, aware that I was powerless over my own life, determined to stay away from the things that were bad for me. Problem was, *I* was bad for me. I made promises I could never keep. I found love, then purposely lost it. As I got deeper and deeper into the groove of my addiction, I repeated the depressing cycle of using and sobriety, using and sobriety, until I hit a wall. By the beginning of 1996 (not long after my affair with Simon Rex), I declared myself celibate. My heart and body had shut down for business.

It was the great sealing of the gates, the self-enforced abstinence of Miss Bobbie Brown. My body was a machine than ran on methamphetamine, not love, not hormones. The army of platonic male friends that I had always kept close at hand were confused and titillated by my chastity—they could look but not touch. I was the whore turned Madonna, the drug-addled virgin mother upon whose bosom they could rest their heads, but between whose legs they could never venture. I was completely unavailable.

As the numb and barren years drifted along, I retreated so deep within myself, and so deep into my addiction, that I almost forgot what it felt like to have feelings for another human being. My life was the same old cycle of highs and depression-filled lows, of trying to be a mother to Taylar, who was now old enough to sense that all was not well, and of running to my own mother back home in Baton Rouge for help.

Then one day in 1999, David Navarro, Mephistophelean guitarist and legendary junkie from Jane's Addiction, came into my life. It had been four years since I had felt anything for any man, but I knew there was something special about him the second I laid eyes on him. He was at Jones restaurant in West Hollywood, sitting with friends. I was at a table nearby. We hadn't been introduced before, so I tried to work out a way to get his attention. I never, ever went out of my way to flirt and catch men's eyes—I always let them come to me. If I ever dated someone, it was because they had chased me down. The fact that I was even trying to get Dave Navarro's attention was unusual for me, possibly a first.

I wandered innocently toward his table, acting like I was looking for someone, hoping he would see me and invite me over. I might as well have been invisible—Dave remained engrossed in conversation with his friends. I couldn't believe it. Later that night, as I left the restaurant, I pulled my car up to the door of Jones. "Will you tell Dave Navarro that Bobbie Brown said to meet her at Grand Ville later?" I asked the doorman, who nodded. I spent the night searching for his face in the club. But Dave never showed up. *Hm.* I wasn't used to being ignored.

A month later, I was home alone, tweaking and scrapbooking like a weirdo, when I got a call from a girlfriend of mine called Linda. She and a few of our friends—Zim Zum from Marilyn Manson's band and a guy called Fairy—had run into Dave at Crazy Girls, our favorite strip bar. "We're going back to his house right now, and he said we should invite you," she said.

"Are you fucking kidding me?" I said, dropping the superglue. "Yes! I'm so there!"

Half an hour later, I was on Dave's doorstep, ringing the doorbell. A few moments later, the door opened. It was Dave, holding a rifle, butt naked except for a pair of sunglasses, a feather boa, and a depraved smile.

"You're the one who tried to get my attention at Jones, right?"

"Right," I spluttered, trying to act cool. I was so embarrassed, though.

"So, I'm downstairs with this groupie chick right now," said Dave, matter-of-factly. "We're taking Polaroids. She's kind of a star fucker. You mind waiting until I'm done? I'll put a video on for you in the meantime."

He led me to a couch in the living room, where Zim Zum and Fairy and a couple of other people were hanging out. Then he squatted in front of the TV, put a video in the VCR, and pressed play before leaving the room. Before me was a series of images showing Dave Navarro jerking off in slow motion. I watched, mesmerized, until this strange man ejaculated on-screen. Right on cue, Dave came back in the room, with the star fucker in tow. I knew she was the star fucker because Dave had put a sticker on her shoulder that said STAR FUCKER. She also happened to be my friend Linda, the girl who had called me. Before I even had a chance to say hello, he walked Linda to the door and showed her out. She didn't look too happy about it.

By this point he was wearing skintight lavender leggings, a leopard-print hat, and the boa. No underwear. "Bobbie, would you like to look at these photos?" He held out the Polaroids he had just shot of himself having sex with my friend Linda. "That's okay," I said, mildly horrified. Dave led me to the kitchen as he brewed some green tea. "So, did you like the video?" he asked. "Oh, yeah," I said without skipping a beat. "I feel like I really know you now." He laughed. "Yeah, it was really cute that you tried to get my attention at Jones," he said, casually picking up the toaster, tying the cord around his arm, and shooting up, like it was no big deal. "What are you doing?" I gasped. Needles made me cringe. He ignored me. "We're going to get married one day, Bobbie," he said, and my heart froze. "Well I haven't had sex in like, four years, so good luck trying," I said, laughing nervously and lighting up a cigarette. This was the trippiest scene I had ever been in. But his eyes softened. "Really?" he said.

All night, he followed me around his little party, pulling me

aside to talk to me whenever he could. Like me, he had no filter when it came to his life stories. "Shortly after I joined Jane's
Addiction, I thought it would be really rock star and cool if I
fucked myself with a dildo onstage," he said. "So I'm playing my
guitar groove with a dildo sticking out of my ass pointing at the
crowd, and I figure I'm going to turn around everyone's going to
be all, 'Check him out, he's so awesome!' But the rest of the band
was looking at me like, 'What the fuck are you doing?' And then
I turn around to an entire audience of people with their mouths
open, not amused. I guess I don't do that anymore."

"Oh my God, what a fucking dork!" I laughed. "Dude,
I would have been horrified too, seeing a dildo hanging out
your butt. There are certain things you don't need to share with
everybody, Dave." He smiled. "You know, Bobbie, it's too bad
you were born with only a charming sense of humor. . . . I
mean, it's a shame God didn't bless you with good looks too.
Because girl, you sure got hit by the ugly stick." Then he broke
into giggles. I stared at him, mesmerized. We talked until the
sky outside broke into one of those magnificent L.A. dawns, the
kind I've seen way more often than I'd like to admit.

CRAZY TOWN

The music scene of the late '90s and early to mid-2000s had
evolved far beyond the hair metal hangover that was under way
when I first arrived in L.A., in 1989. Grunge had come and
gone, ending in 1994 with the death of Kurt Cobain, spawn-

ing a mass of indie rock imitators. New sounds had emerged; the pop-punk of Green Day and Blink-182; the ska-punk of No Doubt and Sublime, and so-called nü metal as typified by rap-rock bands like Korn and Limp Bizkit, who would sell 40 and 30 million albums, respectively. There was the industrial metal of Marilyn Manson, Nine Inch Nails, Ministry, and White Zombie, and the Southern-fried hip-hop of Outkast. The few latter-day hair metal acts that had survived the collapse of the Sunset Strip scene, Guns N' Roses in particular, had grown into household names, and the lesser-known second-wave bands retained a small but passionate underground following.

Being that I was always at the clubs, it was inevitable that I would find myself in contact with the new crop of musicians on the scene. I hung out with the guys in Marilyn Manson's band a bunch and became close with his bassist and guitarist Twiggy Ramirez. We did each other's makeup and posed for heroin-chic photo shoots, photographing ourselves with his fake guns and his headless baby dolls. Twiggy was always gakked the fuck out on coke, and I was always on speed, but we never hooked up. Not only was I celibate, I just wasn't into that spooky Edward Scissorhands look they were rocking.

Jonathan Davis was a quiet kid from Bakersfield, California, who found himself in one of the top-selling bands of the late '90s, Korn. Jonathan liked to hold boys' hands, which made me wonder if he might be bisexual, but he was far from it. When I met him he was married, soon to divorce, and about to meet the love of his life, an absurdly pretty porn star called Deven Davis, whom he met on the road in a strip joint. I first saw them out together at Dublin's, a seedy little rock bar on Sunset. Deven, who actually is bisexual, went bananas for me, wanting to kiss me, flirting wildly, asking me to go home with them. Outside the club she got on her knees and bowed to me and begged for a kiss. "Okay," I said, and we made out on the sidewalk. "That's my wife," said Jonathan, nodding his head, smiling.

Fred Durst from Limp Bizkit was my club buddy; I liked to call him a "back hatter" because he always wore his baseball cap backward. He gave me a hard time for smoking, because he hated cigarettes. "Frankly, I don't *care* what you hate," I would respond, lighting up anyway—and then he would ask me for a cigarette. When the DJ played one of his songs he would always want to go dance, which I thought was kind of cheesy. But Fred didn't care; he was having his moment. One time, at a club, he put his tongue down my throat, catching me completely by surprise. *Nope, I don't think so,* I thought, pulling away. But Fred, for all his tomfoolery, was really smart and full of business savvy. A talented guy who knew what he wanted.

"If we don't find anyone else, in five years we'll get married," said Bret Mazur. Bret was the front man of Crazy Town, and their song "Butterfly" had been topping charts the world over. He and Seth Binzer, his bandmate, had come up with the idea for Crazy Town while writing letters to each other in rehab. Bret had solid rock 'n' roll pedigree—his dad was Billy Joel's manager, and Bret, influenced by West Coast rap, had made beats for Bell Biv DeVoe while still in high school. He was House of Pain's

DJ for a while, and I knew him through Danny Boy and Jay Gordon. Bret and I had a shared natural affinity for hip-hop and a love for partying. He liked the company of pretty girls, and I was looking for that devoted male BFF in my life. We were best friends, the perfect couple that never was. I could tell him anything and everything, and vice versa. Then one day he crossed the line and kissed me. I was so embarrassed I froze him out of my life entirely. But I had warned him. I was damaged goods.

MY RIDICULOUS ROOMMATE

It was the middle of 1999. My constant partying had taken its toll on my career and my bank account, and I was no longer able to afford my cute little town house. It was a cycle that would repeat itself over and over throughout the years. Because as much as speed makes you feel like you're in control, what it's actually doing is robbing your mind of the ability to make sane, rational decisions. You'll brush your teeth for four hours but forget to open your mail. You'll take on home-improvement projects but neglect to pay your rent. Now, thanks to speed, I was thirty years old and about to enter the transient, couch-surfy period of my life, relying upon the kindness of friends (and sometimes strangers) as I ping-ponged back and forth between well-intentioned sobriety and the inevitable relapse into Meth Land.

Tommy Lee had heard I was in trouble, and to my surprise, I found myself on the phone with him, discussing becoming his roommate. It was surreal, and I wasn't sure if my heart could handle it, but beggars can't be choosers. "I just need somewhere temporary until I can get on my feet," I told him on the phone, and he said, "Absolutely, come crash for as long as you need." I asked him if Taylar could come too, and he said sure. *Thank fuck,* I thought, packing up boxes at the town house, breathing a sigh of relief. He and Pamela had divorced a year prior, in 1998, and he had spent time in jail for spousal abuse. I wondered if that experience had made him change. *Maybe this is his way of trying to make things up to me,* I thought.

Tommy was living in a huge house in a canyon close to Malibu. When I arrived, his two kids, Brandon and Dylan, were swimming in the pool. "Oh my God, look at your boys, Tommy!" I gasped. Brandon was very well-mannered, polite and shy, whereas the younger boy, Dylan, was more rambunctious, taking his shoe and beating Brandon with it, acting like a little badass. "He sure reminds me of you," I said, and Tommy laughed.

As surreal as the thought of being roomies with my ex-fiancé was, it was the best (only) option I had, and I was grateful for his generosity. I brought a few suitcases of clothes over and went back to my place to pick up a few boxes before putting the rest of my belongings in storage. When I got back to Tommy's house, I saw that my suitcases had been moved from the hallway.

"I put your stuff away for you," said Tommy.

"Wait, where?"

"In my bedroom."

Indeed, all my clothes and belongings were unpacked and hanging in his closet.

"Why did you do that?" I asked.

"My closet's really big, don't worry about it," he said.

"Well, where am I supposed to sleep? Taylar's coming soon—there's a guest room for us, right?"

"You can sleep wherever you like, Bobbie, don't sweat it. There's plenty of room."

I looked around the bedroom. It was impossible to miss the giant Chinese basket—a hammock-like sex swing—suspended from the ceiling by heavy steel chains. "Um, who's the idiot getting in *that* thing?" I said. "Dude, you know that's kind of cheesy, swinging around with your dick all over the place. What the fuck?" Tommy started cracking up, and it was just like old times again. I sat down on the edge of the bed. This was a lot for me to take in. I still felt intensely attracted to Tommy. But even though my crotch was saying yes, my head was saying no fucking way.

"Tommy, I'm really grateful you're helping me out. I just don't have a dime right now. Maybe I should have made a sex tape—you know, to boost my career." It was an off-the-cuff comment, but Tommy's eyes gleamed mischievously.

"Check this out," he said, walking toward a table with a pile of documents on it. He grabbed something, smiled, and held it up in front of my face. It was a royalty check from the company that had put out the sex tape. The check was for a lot of money, six figures.

"Damn!" I said. "You asshole! So was that shit even for real?"

Something about the tape had always felt contrived to me. Not once had Tommy wanted to film us having sex. Yet after their tape was leaked online in 1996, it seemed like rather than harm Pamela's career, it had made the public even more obsessed with her. When Pamela and Tommy sued the distribution company that had put it out there, Internet Entertainment Group, they were awarded $750,000 for their share of the profits. Not bad for a little home video. Tommy didn't comment but shrugged his shoulders and winked.

This was all too much for me—all I knew was that I was tired and wanted to take a bath. Tommy said I could use his bathroom, which had a huge Jacuzzi.

"That sounds amazing! Thank you, Tommy."

"Of course! I'll be downstairs in my studio if you need anything."

I lay in the tub, submerged in bubbles, and closed my eyes. The roar of the Jacuzzi jets was soothing, and I inhaled the soft scent of vanilla votive candles. My muscles relaxed and my headache disappeared. Finally, some peace and quiet.

"Hey, babe!"

I screamed and opened my eyes. Tommy was crouching next to the tub, holding two shots of Jäger, his head inches from mine.

"Wanna party?"

"No! Get out of here!"

"Oh, okay," he said, pouting, leaving the room, downing both shots.

I was starting to realize that Tommy's inviting me to move in had less to do with his good heart and more to do with his hard dick. He constantly came into my bedroom at night, trying to talk to me, or inviting me to go out with him. Every time, I said no. When I got phone calls, he would act jealous, like he was my boyfriend. To complicate matters, while I was staying with Tommy, Nikki Sixx, his bandmate, had started calling me, inviting me over to talk about his fashion line, which he wanted me to model for. Wisely, I refrained from mentioning anything to Tommy, but curiosity got the better of me and I went to Nikki's house to find out what he had in mind. Well, let's just say it wasn't fashion. As soon as I arrived it was clear Nikki was not sober anymore. Instead of talking clothes, he wanted to hang out and party. So I got high in my way, and Nikki got high in his, while I read his tarot. When he tried to snuggle up to me, I made my excuses and left. What with having already dated Tommy and kissed John Corabi, I was in danger of hitting three-quarters of Mötley Crüe—a dubious accomplishment if ever there was one. (Nikki got back with his wife, Playmate and *Baywatch* star Donna D'Errico, shortly after that.) Meanwhile, life back at Tommy's manor was devolving from cathartic to chaotic. Taylar (who was now eight years old) had arrived, and the two of us were holed up in the guest room that would become our Alamo. I told her I wasn't sure how long we would be staying with "Dad Tommy" this time, and she didn't seem too perturbed—it turned out she too was under attack.

"Mommy, Brandon won't stop following me around," she whispered. Tommy's eldest son had developed a crush on her and was as clingy and demanding as his father, apparently. When Taylar said she felt sick and had to lie down, he would lie next to her saying, "I feel sick too," staring at her with googly eyes, which grossed Taylar out (she was not into boys at all at this point) and caused Dylan, the younger son, to fly into insane fits of jealousy. I was running from Tommy, Taylar was running from Brandon, and Brandon was running from Dylan, who would inevitably be trying to hit him with a shoe. It was madness.

HIDE THE WEENIE

After a week or so of chasing me around his house, to no avail, Tommy finally got the hint. Insulted, he took revenge by inviting random girls over to stay the night, parading them in front of me, perhaps in a bid to rouse some kind of reaction.

"Um, don't mind me," I would say, knocking on the door in the morning, tiptoeing past Tommy and some girl in his bed, so I could get to my sweaters, which remained in his closet, at his insistence.

Then Tommy made things really uncomfortable: "No Weenie in the house," he announced. Weenie was my dachshund, and after Taylar, she was my main squeeze. Tommy said Weenie could stay in the garage, which was not cool with Weenie, who was used to cuddling up in bed with me at night. Taylar and I would sneak Weenie in to sleep with us every night and hide her under the covers until morning. Then Tommy found out (Dylan, we believe, was the informant), and told us Weenie now had to sleep in the car. It felt like Tommy was just being mean, and it was bringing back bad memories of our breakup. Two weeks into our roommate arrangement, I sat Tommy down to talk.

"You know, Tommy, I'm so grateful that you have let us back into your life in this way, but it feels like maybe we've gotten off on the wrong foot." I didn't want to have to put a chair against my bedroom door to stop Tommy from bursting in at night, which he had done a couple times. Of course I was still in love with him. But it didn't seem like his feelings had the same depth as mine. I was starting to feel like some disposable dial-a-girlfriend, a plaything to pass the time with. That was something I could never be, especially not with Tommy. His reaction was less understanding than I had hoped. "If you're not happy, feel free to leave, Bobbie," he said, as cold as he had been playful just a few days earlier. I was crestfallen at the thought of packing up my life again. But it was obvious, yet again, that Tommy and I just couldn't be together. It never seemed to work. And knowing how Tommy liked to keep his exes close, I had a feeling Pamela would be coming around again. Except this time she was still a major star with a solid career, and I was a drug addict part-time model looking for couches to crash on. I doubted Tommy would show me any more loyalty than he had the first time he discarded me for her. *Why on earth would I want to put myself through that pain and humiliation a second time?* I thought. I may have been a fuckup, but I wasn't a masochist.

After leaving Tommy's, me, Taylar, and Weenie stayed at Bobby Hewitt's house for a weekend, and then I sent Taylar back to Louisiana to stay with my mom. I went from house to house for a month or so and stayed at Sharise's for a while, and then went back to Louisiana myself. Because my life and all my "friends" were in L.A., I would bounce back and forth, crashing with people in L.A. and then going back to Baton Rouge as soon as my welcome—or my nerves—wore out. Whichever came first. I was living life day to day, hit to hit, waiting for something, someone to save me.

CHERRY RE-POPPED

I was still celibate. It was like the Ice Age down there—that part of me felt like it had shut down.

In some ways, my sexual hibernation was symptomatic of a deeper illness. It was a defense mechanism in response to the chaos that my life had become. I no longer respected myself. I was couch surfing, in and out of various apartments. I was fucking off at work and not prioritizing. I hated not having a home, not having stability, not being the mother I wanted to be, and I hated that I had had so much and lost it all. When you're carrying around that much self-loathing, it is impossible to feel attractive enough to be genuinely intimate with another person. At least, that's how it was for me. The part of my heart that trusted men enough to be open to them physically had almost completely atrophied. Guys were still pursuing me, and I knew I was still beautiful. But love was no longer something I could even relate to. In many ways, I blamed love for all the pain of the past five years.

Amid the darkness glowed a distant light—Dave Navarro. He had the confidence of Tommy Lee and the intelligent sensitivity of Jani Lane. It was a potent combination. He was damaged, more damaged than I, which made me feel safe somehow. I felt like he understood me. Whenever I was in L.A., I spent time at his place, which, for a junkie's house, was extraordinarily clean and well ordered. In fact, it was very comfortable. The upstairs had a balcony that looked over all of Hollywood. Downstairs was the master bedroom, and when he was coming down off heroin, he would often ask me to just lie with him there because he felt sad. Sometimes we would say the same thing at the same time—it was like we thought the same thoughts. He would have been my perfect boyfriend had we not both been so fucked-up on drugs.

Dave was still deeply affected by the death of his mother, a beautiful blond former model, Constance Colleen Hopkins, who was devoted to her son. She was murdered by her boyfriend, John Riccardi, in March 1983. Dave, who believed in a lot of pagan iconography, felt that unicorns were representative of motherhood and kept many unicorny things around the house. He even had a unicorn sock puppet, which he was very attached to. One time, my brother, Adam, was waiting for me on the couch when Dave, who was hiding behind the grand piano, pranked him with the sock puppet. "Hello," said the unicorn, popping out from behind the piano. My brother nearly jumped out of his skin. The unicorn carried on in a high-pitched warble. "Let's sing a Prince song! *This is what it feels like when doves cry.*" A few days later, Dave showed up at my house with the sock puppet. He snuck around the side of my house to my brother's bedroom window (he was staying with me at the time). My brother heard a tapping on the window and was horrified to see the unicorn was back. Dave had a wicked sense of humor. Had he not been one of the worst junkies I had ever met, I might not have been so hesitant about him. It may sound hypocritical, because I was an addict too, but the needles—they creeped me out.

MY BROTHER, THE MANNY

Adam had moved into my house in the Valley a few months after I befriended Dave Navarro. After graduating high school, he had come for a visit and basically never left. In return for living at my place for free, he took care of Taylar. He was her "manny." He would wake up in the morning and take her to school and I would pick her up in the afternoons. When I was too fucked-up to think straight, Adam would pick up the slack. Taylar loved him, and to this day, they remain close.

Adam knew I was using, but he would never say anything, because he knew how defensive I could be about my addiction.

If I was acting up or acting weird, he would just ignore me or look at me like I was insane and not say anything, and that would normally make me snap out of my crazy behavior for a few minutes.

"I can't feel the top of my left leg—it's totally numb," I complained one day.

"Well, that could be the result of bad circulation due to drug use. But that's not what I'm saying it is."

He had a way of tiptoeing around me if I was fucking up and just quietly picking up the pieces. He has a quiet strength that is so powerful most people never even notice it. I knew that he loved me and had mad respect for me, even though I often felt like the poster child for what *not* to do with your life. Not once did he make me feel judged, although it was obvious that he and Taylar had their doubts about this Dave Navarro character I was so enamored with.

SHOWDOWN

Something about my closeness with Dave was bothering Jay Gordon. Every time I hung out at Dave's, Jay would magically show up. If I talked about Dave, he would change the subject. Jay was just my club buddy, as far as I was concerned, one of the boys in my friend zone. I loved to make Jay the butt of my jokes, and would go out of my way to horrify him. He took himself very, very seriously, which of course only made me tease him more. He had this robotic emo look, all black spiky hair. So I would stick gum on his forehead, spit Altoids at him, and throw quarters at his head—anything to snap him out of his poseurness. We had an antagonistic brother-sister relationship going on. As such I couldn't ever imagine being sexual with Jay. Which is why his jealousy seemed strange. Then the penny dropped. He must be in love with me! I thought it was cute. When was Jay ever going to realize that sex with me just simply wasn't on the cards? Poor thing.

"C'mon, Bobbie, don't you want to sleep with me?" said Dave. "Just think how amazing it's going to feel with me inside you, after five years of nothing." We'd kissed once, and he had played with himself while we did. Dave was all about self-pleasure, and he really loved to masturbate. This was by far the most intimate sexual contact I'd had in a long time. I didn't let him touch me, though. I was tormented. *How can I go from Tommy Lee to everyone, to no one, to a guy doing needles?*

The best trip I ever had on ecstasy was with Dave. I had done ecstasy a million times, and to be honest, I wasn't a huge fan. But one night Dave had some MDMA powder in capsules. I shook my head and shuddered. "No, dude. Every time I do it I don't have that much fun."

"Trust me, Bobbie, it's the best stuff," he said. Grudgingly, I took the pill and waited for the grossness to begin. As I came up, I noticed I wasn't suffering the usual side effects. There was no nausea, no wooziness, no heart palpitations. Just an intense warmth and clarity that filled my heart and focused my vision almost entirely upon Dave. He seemed to be glowing. We roared with laughter about God knows what, finishing each other's sentences. "You're freaking me out!" I giggled as I started a sentence and he finished it, again.

"No, *you're* freaking *me* out," he said.

"Actually, you're freaking *us* out, so go fuck yourselves," said one of Dave's friends, who was also hanging out in the living room with us. It felt like the drug had opened a gateway between my mind and his, and I no longer knew where I began and Dave ended.

That night, after everyone left, we kissed until the sun rose. Dave, of course, couldn't help but touch himself—he is the most masturbatory man I have ever known. But he did not attempt to touch me. For months, we hung out like this at his house. He never tried to press me into going further with him sexually, which made me feel safe. One night, when we were finally alone (there was almost always somebody at his house), we were on the couch and Dave got carried away, putting his hands up my dress. His familiarity was starting to freak me out. Suddenly, having sex with Dave Navarro was starting to feel like a real possibility. I realized he really wanted to take it there. *Do I even know how to have sex anymore?* I wondered. *Is he going to be turned on by me?* My mind became flooded with self-doubt. When I realized that I was on the brink of tumbling into something sexual with Dave, instead of going with the flow, I decided to rob us both of that experience and waste that incredible closeness and buildup we had created.

How?

"Okay, I'm going to try this. Jay, *don't move*. Just do what I tell you, okay?" Having friend sex with Jay was the last thing I wanted to do. But I did it anyway. I couldn't bear the thought of being an out-of-practice sex loser with Dave, so I figured I'd oil up the wheels with Jay. And boy, was it nothing to write home about. In fact, it was over as soon as it started. You must understand, I hadn't had sex in so long, it was like cranking up an ancient machine and hoping that it still worked. It felt mechanical and strange, not romantic at all, and about eleven seconds in, I was done. I rode Jay like a bicycle, letting off five years' worth of steam, and then hopped off when I was finished, glad it was over with. "That was fucked-up, Bobbie, I feel totally used," said Jay afterward. "Well, sure, Jay," I said, ruffling his hair. "Think of it as a favor to a friend." Delighted that my girl parts still worked, I hopped out of bed, and texted Dave, telling him I was coming over.

"Where are you going?" said Jay, looking annoyed.

"To Dave's," I said. I hadn't even showered. But I had just had sex for the first time in five years. The famine was over. Time to go.

"Well, I'm coming with you," said Jay.

"Sure, babe," I said, distracted.

I walked in the door to Dave's house, with Jay on my tail, right behind me. "Bobbie, it's going to be so amazing when we're together," said Dave, pulling me close and kissing me as soon as I walked in the door. He too felt that our time was drawing near. "I'll be your first man in nearly five years."

"First guy in five years? Make that five minutes," Jay chimed in, grumpily. Dave looked confused, and then angry, and then disappointed, as Jay blurted out what had just happened between us.

"Wow . . . okay," said Dave.

"Wait, you don't mind, do you?" I asked him.

Dave had never said that he wanted to have a committed relationship with me or anything like that. He had never said that he was in love with me. So I assumed he wouldn't mind about the Jay thing. He was a rock star. And rock stars don't have feelings. Right?

"Well, congratulations, Bobbie," said Dave. "I hope you both had fun."

We had been hanging out for seven months straight, but after that night, everything changed. He became very detached and unemotional. He wouldn't return my calls or my texts. It was surreal. I wondered if Dave Navarro had been some guy I just dreamed. But no, he was just another guy I had fallen in love with, exploding into my life and disappearing in a puff of smoke, much like the others. *Fuck.*

At least I still had the ever-devoted Jay. One night, he was massaging me on my bed; it felt good to be touched by someone I trusted. "If you ever want to try that thing again . . . let me know," he said, grinding my shoulders with his thumbs. Even though I was pining for Dave, I was more open to Jay's suggestion than I might have been before. "OK," I said, coyly. "What's the harm."

The first time Jay and I had slept together, I had not given him any opportunity to prove his prowess as a lover. This time, he insisted on taking the lead.

"Just lie there, Bobbie, and don't move." He started going down on me and I winced, feeling self-conscious. "Jay, c'mon, you really don't have to." He looked up from between my legs, annoyed.

"Bobbie, you need to just fucking relax. I love doing this and I don't care if it takes hours. Now shut your trap." I had never really been into oral. That night, I learned why. Because no one had ever done it right. I would always pretend to be excited while thinking, *Let's just get to the fucking point.* But that night was the first time I had an orgasm through oral sex. Jay went down on me for hours, making me come three times before even entering me. It was like a whole new world. Now I understood why he had lots of girls in his life; he was blessed with a silver tongue. I couldn't wait to try it again with Jay, even though we were, of course, just friends.

The next day, I felt stronger, renewed. But Dave was still refusing to respond to my messages and apologies. *Fuck him,* I thought, suddenly angry. I was sick of being treated this way.

Hey, Dave, it's okay that you're blowing me off, because I'm seeing someone else anyway, I typed into my phone, feeling triumphant.

Dave wrote back immediately.

You've been seeing someone all this time? You lied to me?

My heart pounded. *Oh, shit. What had I done?*

No, I wasn't really seeing someone, I kind of just said that, I backpedaled. Hearing back from him was such a relief. *Maybe we have a second chance here.*

You're a mess, Bobbie! A mind-fucking bitch! Fuck you!

Maybe not. I was stunned. I tried calling him, but he wouldn't pick up. I kept calling him and calling him and he finally agreed to let me come over. He was so businesslike, it hurt.

"That wasn't cool, Bobbie—you really hurt my feelings," he said, matter of fact. "I don't like you anymore. Why would you sleep with Jay like it didn't even mean anything? That is the dumbest thing I have ever heard."

"Dave, I don't know what the fuck I was doing, I was trying to protect myself. You're a famous rock star. . . . I really thought I just had to play it cool with you."

Dave just shook his head.

"You're not cool, you're over-the-top, Bobbie. You act like yours is the only broken heart in the world."

I had never imagined that any rock star guy could ever be capable of breaking it down like that. Especially not Dave Navarro. The whole seven months we were spending time together, I was caught up in how fucking cool he was, I didn't realize he was, like me, just another fuck up trying to survive and maybe find some real love along the way.

"Listen, Bobbie, I don't even know if we can hang out anymore. I'm sorry."

I drove home, devastated. Guilty. Confused. It didn't seem to matter what I did; I couldn't help but fuck things up. *Nobody fucking loves me,* I thought, a bottomless well of self-pity.

Through my tears, I scrolled through my phone, looking for Jay's number.

Jay had been my friend for so long, I felt safe unloading all my rawness onto him. He had been pursuing me for so long, I assumed he must have been in love with me. All the truths I had been withholding from Dave I dumped straight onto Jay's lap, assuming my open wounds were what he wanted. But Jay was not Dave.

Our decade of friendship, combined with the joy of my sexual reawakening and the transference of my feelings for Dave Navarro, blinded me to the fundamental incompatibilities of Jay Gordon and Bobbie Brown. Of which there were many.

1. We were an odd couple. He was a scene queen who plucked his eyebrows and wore cyber-goth platform boots, PVC, and latex; I was a blond mom who liked hip-hop, Ugg boots, and 'N Sync.

2. He was incapable of committing to one girl; I was used to being the center of every man's attention.

3. He thought I was a big dork; I knew I was a big dork.

4. He wore more makeup than me, yet we couldn't even share foundation—he preferred shades of alabaster, whereas I was always more California tan.

You couldn't find two less compatible people. Until we were in bed.

Even though we saw each other nearly every day, Jay refused to refer to me as his girlfriend. Even after a year of being fuck buddies, I sensed that Jay would bail if I put any pressure on the relationship, and I couldn't bear the thought of being alone. But I couldn't hold back my feelings any longer. He was lying on my bed, and I stood next to it and tapped his shoulder.

"Jay, I love you."

He turned and looked up at me, surprised.

"I'm telling you that because it's how I feel, not because I'm expecting a specific answer back from you," I said, nobly. "Whether or not you can say it back to me doesn't affect how I feel." And then I walked away, and my chest relaxed for the first time in months. *Even if he can't tell me he loves me, I know that he does,* I thought.

Actually, I don't know that Jay ever loved me. He might have said he did once or twice in the five years we would spend together, on and off. But in that moment he just nodded his head and smiled. "That's cool."

The days I couldn't see him were torture, because I sensed he might be with another woman. My obsession grew. I found myself parking my car outside his studio to watch which girls would come in and out, confirming whatever lie I suspected Jay had just told me. Even when he was caught red-handed, he would never be honest, so I would default to believing him. It was easier to believe his bullshit than to accept that yet again, I was alone and addicted to a fantasy. I was convinced I could make him fall in love with me. After all the bullshit I had gone through, the least he could do was *try* to love me.

When I walked in on him in bed with another girl, it sparked my first panic attack. "Bobbie, get the fuck out of here," he hissed, half-asleep. The girl next to him stirred a little. "And stop crying!" he whispered, pushing me out the door. I fell to the ground, hyperventilating.

"I think I'm having a heart attack," I told my friend Dallas, who I had brought along with me. "Hush, honey, you're having a panic attack," she said, holding my hand. "Let's get out of here and find you someplace quiet to lie down." She, along with all my friends, couldn't believe it when I took Jay back, time and again.

Jay had invited me to meet up with him on tour. A psychic had told me not to go, but I ignored her advice and went anyway. Big mistake. We both partied, and after three days of being awake, I was so fucking tired and emotional. We were in San Francisco, and I just wanted to curl up and get some alone time with Jay. But he decided to throw a full-blown after-party in our hotel room instead. There was this girl and that girl and my nerves were so fried by this point, I started to give him attitude. I couldn't believe that my lover, and my friend for so many years, was treating me like just another groupie, in front of everyone. "What's your fucking problem, Bobbie?" he screamed. I was dumbfounded. Jay told me to get on a plane and get the fuck out of there. In the wee hours, not having slept for three days and bawling my eyes out, I made my way to the airport, found a flight, and cried my way home. Jay and I didn't speak for a year. That entire time, my spun mind still obsessed over him, plotting ways to win him back.

I remembered explaining to Jay, back when I had just broken

up with Tommy, how sex between friends really does change everything. I was right. Once you get strung out on your dick, it's over. Done. We're conquered. When I'm with someone, I flatter him, make him feel special, like he's ten men, even if he's not. And that is a mistake, by the way. Do not do that, ladies. Don't ever let him know that he is completely satisfying you, because as soon as you do, it's over. That's what I have learned, every single time. Hey, I am forty-three, and I am *just* figuring this out.

I should have just listened to Taylar. She *hated* Jay. She thought he looked like a cross between Frankenstein and Edward Scissorhands, and was embarrassed to be seen with him. Whenever he tried to talk to her, she would roll her eyes and say, "Ugh." When we asked her to give us some privacy, she would curl up in a ball and refuse to leave the room. One time Jay dropped her off at school for me and she was mortified. "Mom, why did you do that to me? He looks like Frankenscissors and his hair is like a burnt match. Don't *ever* do that to me again!" When he came over to the house wearing his super-high goth platform shoes, with his spiky black-and-white hair and shaved eyebrows, she would look at me as if to say, *Are you fucking kidding me?* I should have trusted Taylar's intuition—it was much more finely tuned than her mom's at that point.

IF YOU WANT MY BODY

Jay and I were going through an off period, during which he had started hanging out with Rod Stewart's daughter Kimberly. Like all of Jay's girlfriends, she was threatened by me, because even when Jay and I weren't *together* together, we were usually still together, and I would usually be trying to win him back. They say keep your friends close and your enemies closer, and Kimberly had suggested hooking me up with her dad, who was single. I wasn't especially keen. Years ago, I had met Rod Stewart at the Roxbury and hadn't been impressed. "Can I get you anything?" he said, leaning on the bar next to me. "Cranberry vodka?" I said. "No, I meant Ferrari, Porsche, Jaguar?" *What a cheesetard,* I thought.

But I was bored, and jealous of Jay and Kimberly, so I agreed to go on a double date with them. I got ready over at Jay's house, and Jay did my makeup; then I showed up with my ex-boyfriend for my blind date with his new girlfriend's dad. Kids, Hollywood is not a normal place. Seriously. But by this point, I had gotten used to the surreal nature of my life.

Rod was in his midfifties and looked a lot older than I remembered. He had recently separated from his second wife, Rachel Hunter, and was sweet and gentlemanly, but I felt very little attraction and made my excuses as to why I had to leave. "Okay, so why don't we go out another time?" he said. "Let's have fun!" When he said "fun" I pictured him running a hot bath naked, looking over his shoulder, smiling, his balls like socks with rocks in them, hanging to his knees. I told that to Jay and he told me to stop grossing him out.

Rod and I met up again with Kimberly and Jay at a club. We were sitting at our table when all of a sudden a whole gang of girls joined us. One was a girl I was not too fond of, because I had heard that she had slept with Jay while we were together. She was sitting right next to Kimberly, and they were joking and whispering. *They're so cunty,* I thought. "I am not sitting at this table with *certain* people," I announced coldly. "Oh, come on, no drama please," said Rod.

"Your daughter is being a total bitch."

Rod tried to ease the tension by being funny. "Feel my thigh," he said.

"No, thanks."

"Go on, feel my thigh—I play soccer."

I prodded his thigh with my forefinger and thumb in three spots. "Yeah, it's really awesome."

"Do you want to go to my place and Jacuzzi?"

Ugh, not the Jacuzzi line. You can't go anywhere in Hollywood without some douchetard trying to get you in his hot tub. I pictured Rod bending over, naked, and puked a little in my mouth.

"Do you think I carry a bikini in my back pocket or something?"

Rod called me a "silly bird" or a "tart" or some English slang word I did not understand. "I don't know what that means."

"It means 'dumb whore,'" said my nemesis.

Rod, desperate to avert the catfight that was about to erupt, whispered in my ear.

"If you want my body and if you think I'm sexy . . ." I couldn't believe this guy was for real.

"I don't know, Rod, perhaps we should get Maggie May and ask her?" I spat. Rod looked at me, appalled. "Actually, I have a better idea."

I got on the table, bent over, and shoved my ass in his face, spilling his drink in his lap. Then I hopped off the table and marched out of the building. *Fuck Rod, fuck Jay, fuck Kimberly, and fuck that other bitch.* If there was one thing I had gotten good at over the years, it was not giving a fuck.

A DEVASTATING BLOW

One day in 2005, I got a phone call from my mom I'll never forget.

"Earl's really sick, Bobbie. You need to come home."

Mr. Earl, thanks to a lifetime of smoking, had been diagnosed with emphysema. My mom suggested I move back home to spend time with him, and to reconsider my future.

"Bobbie, I don't know what's going to happen, but I think that you need a backup plan in your life," said my mom. "Enough of this Hollywood nonsense. I mean, look where it's gotten you." She said I should come home to Baton Rouge permanently, go back to school, and train for another, more stable career, because it didn't look like this whole Tinseltown thing was going anywhere for me now. I surveyed the last fifteen years of my life—a catalog of missed opportunities and bad life decisions. I was even starting to have regrets about divorcing Jani. *Maybe we could have made it work.* I knew I had to move back home and try to remember what was really important, and spend time with Mr. Earl. Taylar and I packed up my car and drove to Louisiana. At age thirty-six, I moved back in with my parents.

Dragging my suitcases up my mom's porch steps, I felt like the world's biggest loser. Stripped of the parties and the velvet ropes, who was I?

"I hear they're hiring at Subway," my mom suggested, and I wanted to cry. I gave my old bedroom to Taylar and slept in a sleeping bag on the porch every night. I remembered those evenings as a teenager, watching the love bugs fry. I never imagined life would bring me right back here, to where it all started. Except this time I was broke, divorced, and lonely.

Following my mom's advice, I enrolled in Aveda esthiology school an hour away and started studying skin care. "Bobbie Brown? You're famous!" my classmates would say, and I would pretend like I didn't know what they were talking about. "She's my cherry pie!" *Ugh.* I was embarrassed by the attention. I didn't want to remember I was Bobbie Brown, the Cherry Pie girl who had it all and fucked it up.

Mr. Earl had been awake for days refusing to lie down because he knew, somehow, that if he did, it would be over.

Finally, exhausted, he told my mom he was going to take a nap. She lay next to him and they slept awhile. His oxygen machine was still on. After an hour or so she got up. Later she went in to check on him again, but he had stopped breathing. My brother was out back, having band rehearsal with his friends, when he heard my mom's screams. Mr. Earl had been on so many steroids, he weighed three hundred pounds, but my brother was like Superman—he lifted him off the bed, onto the floor, and spent forty-five minutes giving him mouth-to-mouth resuscitation while we waited for the ambulance. But Mr. Earl never woke up. Adam called me on my cell. "Bobbie, Mr. Earl died, you gotta come home from school." It was a week before graduation.

My father, Bobby, went with me to the funeral. We held each other as we cried. Mr. Earl had accepted my father back into the family, and when he died, we knew the world had lost a truly kind man. The death of Mr. Earl put things in perspective— you just never know how long anyone is going to be around. I bought my dad a lighter and had it engraved with the words I LOVE YOU, DAD, and gave it to him a couple days after Mr. Earl's funeral. We were at breakfast, and I noticed my dad wasn't eating a thing. "I just don't have an appetite anymore, BJ," he said. "Well, you need to go get checked out," I said. "I refuse to bury you too, Dad."

Bobby seemed to be in a good place in his life. He was running a bar, and I was helping him out on weekends, going to his house and cooking him dinner. For the first time in many years, he and I were bonding. He had a girlfriend with "an ass like a donkey," which he swore was a good thing. We went to the animal shelter together and I helped my dad choose a puppy to adopt—a little Chihuahua that we named Peanut. I'd never before felt this close to my father, who was in high spirits these days, even though he wasn't eating a lot and had lost some weight. He acted like the weight loss was because he was so busy, and gave me money to buy him a whole new wardrobe because he couldn't fit into his old clothes anymore. Upon my insistence, he went to the doctor and afterward called to tell me what the physician had said. When I heard the words "esophageal cancer" I just flipped. *No, not you too, Daddy—you can't be sick too.* My dad backtracked. "Well, they didn't say that I *had* the cancer; they're just running some tests." That weekend he got so sick he had to go to the hospital.

"Are you okay, Daddy?" I asked him, by his bedside.

"Oh, yes, they're sending me home tomorrow because I'm fine," he replied.

They did send him home in the morning—but not because he was better. Because there was nothing they could do. The cancer was too advanced. I went to his house and he didn't look good. He was only eating ice chips. I knew something was very wrong, but he wouldn't tell me the truth. He had told everyone in the family that he didn't want me or my brother to know that he was dying, even though he was puking up his insides all day and night, and was unable to eat any food or drink any water. My dad ended up losing nearly forty pounds in a week.

One night, at around 4 A.M., I woke up. Crying and shaking, I knocked on my mom's door. "Mom, I can't sleep. I just don't understand what's wrong with Dad." She sighed. "Okay, Bobbie, you have to be strong, okay?" And she told me that my father was dying.

The next day, my dad confirmed it. He told my brother and me that he loved us, but it looked like he was going to have to say good-bye soon. "It's okay, Bobbie, don't cry. These ice chips don't taste so bad, you know. Kinda like steak, if you use your imagination." He was in constant pain, and I wanted him to go back to the hospital. But he refused, stubborn old coot. He hated doctors. I had to think of a way to get him back to the hospital, so I told him that if his liver failed, he would almost certainly become mentally retarded. That convinced him to go—he was proud like that, and wanted to have all his marbles right up to the end.

I went back and forth from the hospital every day. Every time I saw him, I would break down in tears and he would yell at me and send me out of the room. My brother was at his bedside around the clock. Then one night at about 4 A.M., my brother called—our dad had passed away singing an old hymn, "I Have Found a Friend in Jesus." Adam was holding his hand. My dad had never been religious until the last few years of his life. "We're in the end-time, BJ," he'd say, and hand me pamphlets. "Okay, Dad, whatever," I'd say.

I was a screaming basket case at my father's memorial. When they projected photos of him on a screen, I howled like a beaten dog. It was impossible for me to mourn my father in a quiet or dignified way. There was so much, too much, left unsaid. Mr. Earl had been dead exactly two weeks—two funerals in a fortnight. "Everyone is dying, Mom, we shouldn't be here anymore," Taylar said to me at the funeral, and I agreed. The next day, we flew back to L.A.

GOING GOING BACK BACK

Hollywood is such an intoxicating place to live. Even small fishes in its big pond can feel bigger and more important than they ever were back home. Problem is, once you leave, there are plenty more minnows waiting to take your place, and by the time you return, it's as though you never even existed. I had been gone a whole year and found myself back at ground zero, sober, and a stranger in the town I had called home for so many years.

My mom and I paid for Taylar to live with a school friend of hers while I figured out where I was going to go. I had a girlfriend who invited me to stay with her, but she kicked me out the first night, saying she needed her space. Bret Mazur kindly let me stay at his house for a few days. Then I went to a hotel, but I was already running out of money. I called Jesse Woodrow, a preacher I knew, feeling desperate. "I don't know what to do," I said, crying. He said he had a friend who had a spare bedroom and that I could stay there for three days, until her mother arrived for a visit. I showed up with my suitcase and broke down. If I didn't figure out a place to go, I would be homeless. For real this time.

The girl I was staying with was dating a guy called Chris Shinn, a talented rock singer who is the lead singer of Live and was once tapped to be lead singer of Blind Melon. He listened quietly to my woes. "You can come stay with me as long as you like, Bobbie, I have an extra bedroom," he said. At that moment, I remembered that angels are real. I hadn't known Chris five minutes, but he agreed to take me in. Taylar came the second night and we lived there with him for a year, rent-free, at his beautiful home in the Hollywood Hills while I got back on my feet (again). It was hard. I didn't have a job. I was only getting $500 a month from Jani (far less than the child support arrangement we had agreed upon), and the house was a forty-minute drive from Taylar's school—sometimes an hour or more if the horrible L.A. freeway traffic was bad. She was often late for school. But we made it work. I cooked, cleaned, and bought groceries, pitching in as best I could. And there was no funny business, ever, with Chris. He was a good friend and a generous and respectful roommate. But still, it wasn't the best environment for my daughter. We were sharing an air mattress in a small guest bedroom, with an even smaller bathroom. We both knew she deserved better. As much as I had been itching to make it to Hollywood when I was her age, she could hardly wait to leave.

In ninth grade, during the period I was living with Chris Shinn, Taylar went to Baton Rouge for the summer to stay with my mother. In late August, as she was preparing to return to L.A. in time for the new school year, Hurricane Katrina hit. She wasn't able to leave the state in time to start school, so my mom convinced me to have her enroll in high school in Baton Rouge. Not long after, Taylar called, telling me she wanted to stay there permanently. She liked her new friends in school, Runnels, and she liked the stability that living with my mom afforded her. My mom had remarried, and her third husband, Bill Williamson, doted on Taylar. I was devastated, but I couldn't blame her for leaving. She had been bouncing back and forth for so many years, it must have been tiring. Taylar, having witnessed the vain excesses of Hollywood firsthand, had no interest in following in the footsteps of either her mother or her father.

Gifted with words, she wanted to be a novelist, and when she graduated, she went on to study creative writing in college. She is extraordinarily talented, just like her father. When she left, I had to fully face the fact that I had not been the best mother I could have been. I had always dreamed of being the mom who threw slumber parties for her kid, who baked cookies and was in a happy union with her child's father. I knew Taylar deserved all those things. I remembered berating my own mother for falling short in ways that seemed so insignificant, compared with the ways I had failed Taylar. It made me feel ashamed. I had never intended for my daughter to suffer at the hands of my fucking emotional health. But she had. I'm just grateful she turned out as strong as she is.

LET'S BE FRIENDS

Jani, from what I heard, was still on a downward spiral, his alcoholism out of control and his marriage in tatters. He and I talked on the phone occasionally, but his presence in Taylar's life was minimal. He called me from his home state, Ohio, where he had moved with Rowanne. "*Celebrity Fit Club* called and said they want me to be on the show," he said. "I'm not sure, what do you think?" Rowanne was against the idea, but I thought it might benefit Jani. "You should *totally* do it," I told him. "It will revive your career, and the general public will be interested in you again. Plus, they're offering you $80,000. That's eighty thousand more dollars than you had before." He took my advice and moved back to L.A. to film the show. The show's producers even had me film a little clip, wishing Jani good luck. Taylar was visiting, so she and I sat down to watch the first episode together, excited that Jani was finally making a comeback.

"Oh my God, Mom, is that even him?" said Taylar. Jani was performing some songs on the show, and he was barely recognizable to us. Bloated from the alcohol, he seemed disoriented and kept forgetting his lyrics. When he saw the little clip of me wishing him good luck, his response was, "I used to hate her." Taylar and I were worried, and I called him so we could meet and talk. It was the first time we had seen each other in years.

"I'm a fuck up, huh, Bobbie?" said Jani. He was ashamed that the cameras had captured him and his alcoholism, and that the whole world had seen. He told me that he had drank pretty much throughout his marriage to Rowanne, and that she had been a heavy drinker too. He was ready to start over.

With Jani back in L.A., we were able to rebuild our friendship. Enough time had elapsed that we could let bygones be bygones and focus on trying to be better parents to Taylar. Thankfully, by the end of his time on *Celebrity Fit Club*, he had sobered up again and was upbeat—he had actually won the show. And things were good between us; we were talking on the phone nearly every day.

Once again, he brought up the idea of him and me getting back together, but I said it would be impossible. Although I loved him as the father of my daughter and as my friend, I could not imagine being with him romantically again. He took it hard. Jani never was good at being alone.

THE NEW NORMAL

In 2006, for the first time in my adult life, I got a job. Like, a regular job, not one that involved pouting in front of cameras, dancing on podiums, or wearing a bikini. As an office assistant at Le Paws, a pet talent agency, I was responsible for answering phones, running errands, cleaning the kitchen, and refilling the watercooler. I was starting from the bottom. The cool thing about that was, the only way was up.

I went out here and there, and tried to make the scene, but everything was different. Maybe it was my quieter attitude, maybe it was because I was older, but people were less interested in me. In my youth, men would flock to me without me even having to try, and I would just roll my eyes. Guys had offered me $100,000 to spend an evening with them, like that movie *Indecent Proposal*. Which I thought was the creepiest thing ever. "If I could only turn back time," I muttered, as I sent faxes and swept the floors at Le Paws, wishing I had $100,000 in the bank for Taylar and me. I had always been an attractive girl who wasn't aware of her attractiveness and how it could get me places. I tell my friends who are younger than me, "Take advantage of your looks!" Because that shit gets you everywhere. Nine times out of ten, you are getting out of that speeding ticket, or getting to the front of that line, because you are a pretty thing. Girls, be grateful if you were blessed with good looks. Don't be an obnoxious, self-entitled diva, as I was, because baby, your days are numbered.

Jani would often come over and spend time with Chris, Taylar, and me in the evenings. Finally, it seemed like we were both settling into our lives in L.A. Jani as a sober musician, and me as Bobbie Brown, the former model who had a regular job, a regular life, and finally, a little stability. Jani would come pick me up for lunch at work almost every day, and tell me how he was so happy to be able to hit high notes again. I hadn't seen him so happy in a long time, even though he was still troubled by dark thoughts. He had a feeling that he was being followed, and spoke of a darkness in his soul. I put him in touch with

Jesse Woodrow, my preacher friend who is a spiritual advisor (and an actor, of course—this is L.A.). It seemed like Jani could use some guidance.

One night, Jani told Taylar and I that his manager, Obi Steinman, was trying to book him on a major tour, and he was excited about it. But I thought it was a terrible idea. Even though he had been sober a few years, it just seemed too early in his sobriety for him to be going back out on the road and playing shows, surrounded by booze and women and all the things that had fucked him up in the first place. But he didn't listen to me, and in 2008 he went out on the road again, performing solo on an all-star bill with a bunch of other '80s rock bands.

I tried calling him while he was on the road, checking up to make sure he was okay, and he wouldn't take my calls. I hadn't heard anything from him in two weeks when I got a Google alert and it was about him: A producer on the tour had posted all these terrible stories about Jani. How he had fallen off the wagon; how he had flown someone out to perform an exorcism on him; how he dove into a river so he could cleanse his soul; how he hit a guy and told him to suck his dick. All these drunken antics. *What the fuck? This sounds like a bad movie.* I read how he stunned fans in Las Vegas by performing so drunk he was slurring his words, stumbling around onstage, doing Christopher Walken impressions and throwing his mic at a fan.

I called my Jesse, who I assumed was the guy Jani had flown out to perform an exorcism. "Is what I've been reading true?" I asked him, trembling.

"Yes, I'm sorry, Bobbie."

Jesse told me Jani was acting like he was possessed by demons, so much so that Jani's assistant quit and became a devout Christian shortly after the tour. Shocked as I was, things were slowly starting to make sense. Whatever these demons were, real or imagined, I realized that they were the reason Jani was using alcohol. Booze was the only thing that could silence the voices in his head. But the silence came at a price.

Jani was arrested in June 2009 for crashing into a parked car while drunk and was given a misdemeanor DUI and put on probation for three years. In 2010 he was arrested for driving drunk again, and this time, he went to jail for 120 days. He put out a statement to the press: "Anyone out there dealing with personal problems . . . the consequences do not get lighter. I can only say I've never regretted a good decision or action and never been proud of bad ones. People have an astounding ability to forgive. . . . I have to start with forgiving myself."

A SECOND CHANCE

A TV production company showed up at Le Paws one day—they were shooting a reality series about the pets and their owners, but after a few weeks of listening to my motormouth and my insane Hollywood stories, the crew decided to turn the cameras on me. "You need your own show, Bobbie, you're just too funny not to be on television," one of the producers told me. I felt shivers up and down my spine. I liked being *funny*;

funny seemed more substantial than just pretty. There was lon-gevity in being funny, pride to be taken in making people laugh. Since returning to Los Angeles following the death of my two dads, broke and near homeless, with no direction to go in, I'd stopped hinging all of my hopes and dreams on my physical appearance. Those days, I knew, were over. "Really? You think I could do reality TV? I mean, how do we even go about doing that?" I asked. We shot a pilot for a show called *Cougar*, which didn't get picked up. I was crestfallen but excited to be in front of the camera again. I told myself that if the whole TV thing didn't work out, I didn't need to be upset about it. I was still working at Le Paws and it was fun, even though I occasionally got in trouble for being a loudmouth. Life was simple, and I liked it that way.

FINALLY . . . CLOSURE

Every three years, like a comet or a distant planet, Tommy would come around and inject a little chaos into my world. He would reach out to me out of the blue, then e-mail and talk and then maybe we would hang out. Inevitably he would kiss me and tell me he loved me, but never initiate sex. It was as though he was waiting for me to give him the okay to take my body again, but I never did. Eventually, he would leave to go on tour or start dating somebody, or I would start dating somebody, and we would fall out of touch. Then a few years later it would start again. "I can't believe you're dating someone who treats you like shit, Bobbie," he would say, eyes full of concern, as I complained about Jay, or whoever else I was allowing to mess with my head. The irony was not lost on me—no one had broken my heart like Tommy had broken my heart.

"Hey, why don't you come with me to this DJ thing I'm doing?" said Tommy.

"Sure," I said, immediately wondering which of my girlfriends to bring as cockblocker. It was 2008, and I was a year shy of my fortieth birthday. Time sure had flown by, but even after all these years, I still preferred not to hang out with Tommy alone. I still had too many unresolved feelings for him.

Tommy picked us up in a limo, and we headed to the venue. Tommy's driver was chatting with us. "I hear Tommy used to be so in love with you, Bobbie, but then you had a silly fight and broke up." Tommy laughed. I couldn't believe it. Was his driver really making light of how we broke up? After the show, I confronted Tommy. "What you did to me, marrying Pamela like that, was worse than death," I told him. "You *broke* me, Tommy Lee." I laid it out for him, the revenge fucking, the drugs, the rock bottom that my love for him had led me to. Tommy seemed surprised, and then sad. "Listen, Bobbie—I'm really sorry I did that to you, Bobbie. I really am." In that moment, some of the anger and hurt I had been carrying around melted away. Finally it was all, quite simply, in the past.

After that night, Tommy stopped trying to be sexual with me. I think once he understood just how vulnerable I was, he realized it simply wouldn't be fair to make light of my emotions. Even for a big kid, Tommy was starting to grow up. It was a little sad, realizing that he probably would no longer be contacting me every few years anymore.

Chapter Eleven

APPETITE FOR RECONSTRUCTION

The last few years of Jani's life were unbearably painful, not just for him, but for all of us who loved him. Terrified of the people who he thought were following him, and haunted by his fears and paranoia, he sank back into his alcoholism and would never fully emerge. In 2010, I got a call from his on-off girlfriend Sheila Lussier, with whom he was living with in Woodland Hills. She said Jani was having a meltdown, that he was asking for me. I drove over there as soon as I got off work at Le Paws. By now, everyone in Jani's life was accustomed to his alcohol-related breakdowns. But this one seemed different.

I pulled up outside Sheila's house, and Jani shuffled out the door. He wanted to get in the car with me. "Listen, I am *not* taking you to get alcohol," I said, irritated. I felt bad for him, but boozing wasn't about to start solving his problems now. He looked terrible. He was bloated, and his hair was unkempt. His hands quivered on his lap, and his skin was waxy. "Just drive. *Drive!*" he screamed. *Whoa,* I thought. He was scaring me. Even though I had known Jani for nearly twenty years, I had never, *ever* seen him this out of control.

"Take me to the liquor store, Bobbie."

"No fucking way, Jani. Why are you killing yourself? People love you. You have fans, a career, you're talented."

He was sobbing, punching the roof of my car. I begged him to stop. I had seen him sloppy, emotional, needy, incontinent, puking, incoherent—you name it. But I'd never seen him this angry.

"Jani! Will you tell me what the *fuck* is wrong with you?"

"I can't! You'll stop loving me. You stopped loving me before, remember."

"No, Jani, I just couldn't deal with the cheating. You know that."

"Okay, just be quiet and let me speak!"

I sat in silence as, between sobs and punching the window of my car, he told me the secret he had been carrying around for more than twenty years. He was nineteen when it happened. It was after a show. An older man, a major rock star, had invited Jani to hang out with him and the big guys. Jani was young, and easily impressed. Later that night, along with an accomplice, that major rock star put Jani through an ordeal he had been too ashamed to talk about until this moment. It was violent. It was ugly. It was exploitative. Jani said he had been too scared to tell anybody and had been pushing the memory under the carpet, pretending it wasn't there. Jani was a proud man and hated to think of himself as a victim. Now, finally, I understood why he had been acting like one for so many years.

I started to cry.

"You have to do something, Jani. Can't we tell somebody?"

"No, it's embarrassing."

"Fuck that!"

"It would be humiliation for life," he sobbed. "And that motherfucker knows it. That's how he gets away with it. They lie to these young guys who are trying to make it in the music industry, invite them to their show, and they pull this shit. They get away with it because nobody who is trying to make it is going to fuck with them. Nobody."

I helped him back in the house and drove home alone, crying the whole way. I couldn't believe that he had been carrying this around with him for so long. I couldn't believe that there was nothing I could do. I kept quiet about what Jani had revealed to me. And Jani and I never discussed it again.

After Sheila and Jani broke up, Jani moved into his own house with his daughter Madison. There was a spare room at Sheila's and because, as usual, I was looking for a new place to live, Sheila invited me to crash with her. Which is how I found myself living with my ex-husband's ex-girlfriend. Strange but true. Things were tough for me again—I had been fired from my job at Le Paws for calling my boss a dick. The *Cougar* pilot had done little for my career, and now I didn't even have my "normal" job to rely on. I really needed a break.

Sheila told me someone from VH1 had contacted her, trying to find women to interview for a documentary about the Sunset Strip. "You should do it!" she said.

I went for an interview at VH1, and shortly afterward, the

show's producer called me saying they wanted to change the entire idea to focus on the rock star wives. Would I be interested in narrating and helping with the script? "Of course," I said. *Do It for the Band: The Women of the Sunset Strip* aired in 2011, and I guess I made some kind of an impression because Lorraine Lewis, former front woman of the all-girl hair band Femme Fatale, contacted me on MySpace after it aired. "I have always been your fan, Bobbie. I think you are a star, and I was friends with Jani back in the day. I saw you on VH1 and I have an idea that I think you would be perfect for."

I scheduled a lunch meeting with Lorraine and her partner, Lisa, and they told me about their idea. A reality show, starring me, Sharise Neil, Heidi Mark (another ex-wife of Vince Neil's, who would, at the last minute, be replaced on the show by Tommy's sister, Athena Lee) and Blue Ashley, ex-wife of Warrant's Jerry Dixon. The show would be called *Ex-Wives of Rock* and would document the real ups and downs of us former mistresses of the Sunset Strip.

"I love it!" I said, imagining how much fun it would be to reunite with the girls. Amid all the drama that had occurred in our lives, Sharise, Athena, Blue, and I had lost touch. Luckily, all the girls were on board. It had been a long and winding road, but the ex-wives were reunited and ready to rock.

Finally, our lives seemed to be on the up. Jani was sober again and had remarried, and Taylar and I were obviously delighted about that. Jani's new wife was Kimberly Nash, whom he had known since the Warrant days (they had dated briefly after he and I split, then when he married Rowanne, Kimberly was busy having a baby with Warrant's keyboard player. Now, years later, they had rekindled). I would regularly visit at Jani and Kim's home, and things seemed to be going well. We spent Thanksgiving 2010 all together as the funny, disjointed family we had become. Taylar, who was living full-time in Louisiana, had flown into town with her boyfriend, and together with my brother, Adam, we all went over to Kim and Jani's home, and Jani cooked Thanksgiving dinner. He actually seemed happy, for once. That was the last time I would see him alive.

He had been sober nearly two years when Kim called and said he had started drinking again. And it was worse than ever before. He was falling, injuring himself, because he was so disoriented. The alcohol had destroyed his ability to look after himself or those around him. In July 2011, Jani called me, distraught. Things were not going well with Kim, and he asked me if he could move into my downstairs guest apartment. I told him no, the apartment was in poor condition, plus I had a boyfriend who might not be comfortable with my ex-husband moving in with us. Oddly, that seemed to amuse him.

"You have a *boyfriend*? That's hilarious, Bobbie. You haven't had a proper boyfriend in forever."

"Shut up, Jani!"

It was a moment of levity in a year of darkness.

MY SWEET CHERRY PIE

Looking back, the writing was on the wall. Jani was going to rehab every other month, getting sober and then getting drunk, trying to leave his wife and then going back. He had started seeing his ex-girlfriend Sheila again, in between going back and forth with Kim. His life was a mess, and even Jani knew, perhaps, that he might not be able to clean up again this time.

His decline was hard on all of us, but especially Taylar. After our divorce, Jani hadn't been around much, probably because of all the bitterness he harbored toward me. Jani did pay child support but never gave Taylar much beyond the bare minimum, and me, my mother, and Mr. Earl had been almost entirely financially responsible for her when it came to saving up money for college and other expenses. Jani tended to spend money on himself and on his binges, and for years, he hadn't had much time for Taylar. He had been diagnosed with bipolar disorder, and of course he had his well-documented battles with alcohol—as much love as he had for her in his heart, his demons had consistently prevented him from ever being truly there for Taylar.

By the time Jani started reaching out to her, during the last five years of his life, Taylar was still angry with him. "Taylar, you don't understand, people keep giving me alcohol, and I'm helpless against it," he would say, trying to explain his problems. But Taylar wouldn't stand for his excuses. "Come on, Dad. You have to be accountable for your own actions," she would say.

Jani missed her terribly. He had written a song dedicated to Taylar called "Stronger Now" and had gotten a heart and banner tattoo that said DADDY'S GIRL. Jani often called Taylar when he was drunk, to tell her that he loved her, promising her that he would get sober. Of course, he was never able to fulfill the promise for any length of time, and Taylar, now nineteen, had had enough. She felt like the best way she could help her father was by showing him tough love.

"Dad, don't contact me anymore if you're drunk," she told him. "I will only talk to you if you are sober." I understood where she was coming from. But I wasn't sure it was the right approach, somehow. "You know what, Tay, you never know how long your dad will be here," I told her. "He's reaching out to you. He feels really guilty, and he does love you." I felt that Jani only felt able to open up emotionally and let go of his ego when he was drunk. "Drinking is the only way he knows to remove his filter," I told Taylar, and she nodded.

On August 11, 2011, I was taking a nap, half-asleep, floating between dreamland and consciousness. I felt someone move my hair out of my eyes and touch my face. I thought it was Damon, my boyfriend. "Stop, baby, you're waking me up," I groaned, eyes still closed. Slowly, I woke up, charged with an inexplicably sad panic. I looked around for Damon and he wasn't there. I called him, crying.

"What's wrong with you?" he said.

"I want us to be good to each other, always. Life is so fleeting, Damon. What if something happens to you?"

"Babe, I'm fine, we're fine. I'll be home soon."

"Wait—you weren't just here touching my face and hair?"

"No, I left the house hours ago."

At almost exactly the same time, Jani was dying. His wife, Kim, called me the next day with the news—Jani had been found dead of acute alcohol poisoning at the Comfort Inn hotel in Woodland Hills. The cleaner found his body. Someone had checked him in, not under his name, the night before. He didn't have a driver's license or a phone with him. The DO NOT DISTURB sign had been left on the door. I asked Kim if I could go with her to the hotel, where his body was, and she said no. Then I hung up. The next call I made would be to Taylar.

How do you tell a teenage girl that her father, who she has just started building a relationship with, has killed himself with alcohol? What words could possibly lessen the blow? It wasn't fair that this had to be Taylar's reality. I had been blessed with not one but two fathers, both of whom I had achieved genuine love and closeness with. I was glad that Taylar had at least been able to build some relationship with Jani, no matter how strained it had been.

She was in her car, driving to her home in Baton Rouge, when I called.

"Taylar, I'm so sorry, but your dad died yesterday."

"What?" She thought she hadn't heard me right. "What did you say, Mom? I'm driving I can't really hear you."

"Pull over," I said, and I repeated the words. She was in shock. For a few moments, she didn't speak at all. Eventually, she whispered, "Let me call you back."

"Are you okay?"

"Yeah." And then she hung up.

Earlier that day, she had been looking through old photos of her and Jani and had laid them out in her bedroom so she could figure out which ones to take to her new apartment. Jani's smiling face, strewn across the carpet. Her father, whom she so resembled, was dead. We cried together on the phone. "At least I'll see him every day when I look in the mirror," she said.

To this day, the circumstances surrounding Jani's death remain unclear. He had completed his will and divorce papers and was waiting for them to be notarized when he died. Somebody had checked him into the hotel under an alias, and we do not know who that person was. He did die of ethanol poisoning, but at least one other person was present. I would like to find out who that was.

The news of Jani's death came in the middle of filming the first season of *Ex-Wives of Rock*. Because it is a reality show, the cameras captured some of what happened. Not for the first time in my life, I was grateful for the support of my longtime friends. Because no matter how self-destructive Jani had been over the past few years, I never once imagined he would die so soon. He was forty-seven years old, and his death left a huge hole in our lives. Jani had defined the most precious period of my youth, and our love had produced the most important person in my life—Taylar. I had always hoped and prayed that Jani would be strong enough to survive himself, in the same way I had said the same prayers for myself. In the end, though, prayers just weren't enough.

Athena Lee was a great support to me in this time. She had become one of my closest friends thanks to the show, which had allowed us to rekindle the friendship that we started nearly twenty years prior, when I was dating Tommy and living in Malibu.

Athena held my hand through the tears, helping me stay as strong as I could for Taylar. She told me she felt like she wasn't that far behind Jani, because of her own struggles with alcohol. She had already lost her mother and her father, her husband had left her for another woman, and her breast cancer had come back, temporarily. Since she and Tommy are no longer close, I became like family to Athena, and she to me. Now, more than ever, we needed our friends to help us through such trying times.

I'm a very different Bobbie Brown now from the Bobbie Brown she met in Malibu. Back then I was colder, tougher, and more prideful. These days, I'm much more of a softy. I tear up at dog food commercials, for crying out loud. Tough and sassy as I may appear on the outside, I am the biggest fucking wimp in the world, a side of me that came out after my dad died, and after Jani's death too. For so many years, my life had been a whirlwind, decisions fueled by this unearned sense of ego, by this anger at the men who were constantly letting me down. The Bobbie Brown who would act out because of her anger was reckless, foolhardy, and arrogant. It took some very traumatizing experiences to steer me off that path. Today, I know what's really important to me. It's not revenge. It's not drugs. Its not fame or money. It's friendship and family. That's it. And when the time came for me to let go of my relationship with Damon, Athena was there to help me mop up the tears.

I'm proud that Athena, Sharise, Blue, and I are taking the scars we earned on the Sunset Strip and are showing them off to the world. Why not? We aren't rich housewives living in mansions, fighting over Louboutin shoes. When the rock 'n' roll dream fantasy died in the 1990s, it sent us spinning in different directions. Yet somehow, we find ourselves back together, living real lives, complete with beat-up cars and bad decisions. When the show started, I was ridiculed by people for being too real—being overweight, not looking as hot as I used to, having a messy house, or shooting scenes with no makeup on. Well, *whatever*. Yes, maybe I looked like shit. But guess what, that was *real*. Of course, it's no fun reading online that some anonymous asshole in Indiana thinks you're a "stupid skank ho." It's amazing, the people who hate you right out of the gate. They hate us because we were married to rock stars, which is not a realistic or fair reason to hate on anybody. You cannot judge a person without knowing what they have been through.

When Tommy found out Athena and I were doing *Ex-Wives of Rock*, he was not impressed. "I can't believe you and my sister are doing a fucking reality show," he said. "I thought you were smarter than that." He tried to talk us both out of it, probably because he was worried about me and my big mouth. But the show isn't about the rock stars we dated and married. It's about us, as women, today. I think he gets it now. It took my poor mom a second to come around to the show too, especially because in her opinion, I seemed hell-bent on airing all my dirty laundry, in front of all the people of Canada and America.

"That girl has no filter!" she growled to my brother, Adam. "I'm so hurt. I've had enough of it!"

Adam, ever the diplomat, advised me on how to handle the crisis.

"Don't worry about it; I'll talk to Mom while I drive her to her hair appointment. While we're out, leave her a voice mail on the landline saying that you're sorry. By the time we get home, she'll be receptive, I promise you."

Worked like a charm. My brother, who now works in television in Hollywood, is a natural-born superhero.

It took a minute, but my mother came around to her daughter's new career on TV. And I'm proud to be an Ex-Wife. I'm no one's trophy babe, no one's sidekick, no one's punching bag anymore. I'm not hiding behind someone else, nor am I lost in the shadow of anyone else's fame. This time, perhaps for the first time in my life, it's just me being me. I can't tell you how refreshing it feels to say that. And every time I start doubting myself, or start feeling like I might want to slip back into bad habits, I remember Jani. I remember how lucky I am to still be here. And I remember that our daughter needs me.

LETTING GO

Throughout the years Pam and Tommy were together, interviewers would often tell me things that she had said about me, trying to trick me into a reaction. "What do you think about Pam?" they would ask. "I *don't* think about Pam," would be my response. I was lying of course. Not caring, or pretending not to care, was the only way I could think of to cope with what had happened.

I was at a Playboy Mansion party one year when I spotted her, a whirl of peroxide and hangers-on. As I walked past, Pamela and her group of friends started laughing really loudly. They were making fun of me. I paused and looked Pamela in the eye. "Grow the fuck up," I said. And at that point, I realized I no longer cared. We are both in our forties now, for crying out loud. I haven't run into her since then, but I have seen her on television, and I admire her at this point—she's still beautiful and, let's face it, she got everything she wanted. Kudos to her. It's not a competition anymore. I mean—it never really was, until she started going after Tommy.

Tommy was the dirty rocker boy I had spent so many years dreaming about. To this day, I can't believe that the handsome face I pinned on my walls as a lovestruck teenager became the face I woke up next to, for one short, tumultuous year in the mid-1990s. As my momma always said, "Be careful what you wish for." Maybe I should have listened to her. Because when it comes to boys, especially the kind you see roaming up and down the Sunset Strip, Momma is always right.

She always liked Jani, though, despite his damage. We all knew that beneath the rocker façade beat a huge and tender heart. Even though he's gone, I still feel Jani with me every day.

Sometimes I get mad at him for dying, until I realize it wasn't entirely his fault. I'm grateful I got a second chance at life. Jani could have had one too, but his wounds were, it turns out, even deeper than mine. And hopefully Jani's friends and fans will always remember him as he was, an incredible talent, a true star. I really feel like he's watching us. If he is, I hope he knows—cherry pie will always be my favorite.

ACKNOWLEDGMENTS

Thanks to Adam Chromy for his belief in me and my story. To Caroline Ryder, thank you for "getting me" and knowing me so well, which made writing this book a breeze and so much fun. And thanks to Jeremie Ruby-Strauss and Emilia Pisani for making this book a reality. And to Jim Kuzmich. . . . I love you all.

Hey guys,

You've just read some crazy shit, but guess what—this isn't a sob story. This is the tale of a perpetual self-saboteur—me—who, thanks to ignorance, youth, and naivety, ended up trapped in a never-ending life lesson. It took me longer than most to put those lessons behind me, and now that I have, I am grateful daily for the person I became because of those experiences. My past made me a person who is able to listen, help, and support others. My past humbled me, and taught me kindness. It made me aware that life is fleeting.

They say "what doesn't kill you makes you stronger," and that's an understatement as far as my life is concerned. But the strength I've gained is soft at its core. I don't judge myself or the people who have been in my life. Having spent so many years trying to not feel and not to care, I am now a person who feels everything, and who cares. I care a lot.

Thanks for letting me just rip that. LOL.

Love, Bobbie